DATE DUE 4/89

The Stourhead Landscape

Wiltshire

KENNETH WOODBRIDGE

THE NATIONAL TRUST

Acknowledgements

The following have kindly permitted
reproductions of paintings or drawings in their
possession: The British Museum, Francis
Nicholson's views of Stourhead; the British Library
for drawings by S.H. Grimm; Fogg Art Museum,
Harvard University, John Constable's *At Stourhead*;
National Gallery, London, Claude Lorrain's
Aeneas at Delos; Royal Academy of Fine Arts,
Stockholm, drawings by F.M. Piper; Victoria and
Albert Museum, C.W. Bampfylde's drawings of
Stourhead; The Metropolitan Museum of Art,
Purchase, Joseph Pulitzer Bequest, 1917,
[17.50. 17-85], Salvator Rosa's *Tiber and Aeneas*.
Mr D.J. Sales and Mr W.A. Lord, the National
Trust's gardens advisers, have corrected the
presentation of the tree lists and added the
reference numbers to correspond with their
Mature Trees in the Stourhead Landscape.
I am grateful to Mr Dudley Dodd for his interest in
promoting this new edition of *The Stourhead
Landscape*. I am also indebted to Mr Fred Hunt,
head gardener at Stourhead; and to Miss Beverley
Woods for checking the tree lists and providing
additional information on planting dates.

Cover: Watercolour of a view of Stourhead from
the village of Stourton by Francis Nicholson,
British Museum (*Photo John Freeman Ltd*)

Designed by James Shurmer

Printed by The Stellar Press Ltd

Contents

Preface to the new edition   *page 4*

Introduction   *5*

The Making of Stourhead   *12*

Transformations: 1791–1946   *29*

The National Trust and
Conservation   *42*

Plan of the Pleasure Garden   *44*

Buildings, Sculptures and other
Monuments   *45*

Planting 1741–1946   *61*

Selected Stourhead Bibliography   *71*

The Stourhead Landscape

Preface to the new edition

The purpose of this new edition is first to extend the essay on the making of Henry Hoare's landscape garden, since the detailed account in *Landscape and Antiquity* (Oxford, 1970) is now out of print; secondly, to incorporate new thinking on the subject, especially since the publication of the National Trust's report on 'The Conservation of the Garden at Stourhead' (1978). The catalogue of buildings, sculpture and other features has been rewritten in extended dictionary-style entries, giving more information about precedents. The analysis of planting records in the earlier edition contained many species which are no longer represented at Stourhead. This section has therefore been revised, with short accounts of the contribution of each owner up to 1946, and lists which include only those trees at present growing in the garden. Finally, the illustrations have been changed; some omitted and others added. It is hoped that the revised *Stourhead Landscape* will be of value to students of garden history and landscape design generally, as well as to visitors to Stourhead.

K.A.S.W. 1982

Introduction

Origins

From the western scarp of the Wessex chalklands there extends a wedge-shaped plateau, the watershed of the Brue (which flows into Somerset), the Wylye (giving its name to Wiltshire), and the Dorset Stour (which has its source in a valley known as Six Wells Bottom). Nearby is the small village of Stourton where, from before the Conquest, stood the manor house of the Stourtons, on whose arms the Springs of the Stour were represented, 'sable, a bend or between six fountaines'. In 1448 Sir John Stourton, who was treasurer of the royal household to Henry VI, was granted a licence to enclose a thousand acres of pasture, meadow and woodlands 'to impale and make thereof a park'. This included the valley with the sources of the Stour, where at some time the infant stream was dammed to form a series of ponds; and, where it opens out to converge with another valley, two pieces of water, later combined to form the lake.

During the seventeenth century the ancient family of Stourton suffered from being Royalist and Catholic. Their house was sacked by Parliamentary troops during the Civil War, and the estate was encumbered with debt. It was offered for sale in 1704 at £11,000, 'a noble large house in a most pleasant Country having all the advantages of Fine Gardens Orchards Groves Park Warren Fishponds strong large and convenient Dairyhouse Barnes Stables Outhouses and the Desmesnes lying all round it'. It passed to Sir Thomas Meres in 1714, whose son sold it in 1717 for £14,000 to the trustees of Henry Hoare, the banker, second generation of a rising financial elite. Stourton

The arms of Stourton

House, Great Oar Meadow and Six Wells Bottom. (*Aerial photo J.E. Hancock, 1968*)

House, according to Aubrey in 1685, was very large and very old, but 'little consider-able as to architecture'; not only was it inconvenient, but probably, after the neglect it had suffered, uninhabitable. In 1718 it was being pulled down, and under the influence of Henry Hoare's kinsman and brother-in-law, William Benson, a new house was built nearby designed by Colen Campbell in the Palladian style (only the second of its kind), comprising the centre block of the present house, without the portico. It was named Stourhead. To the east was a railed forecourt with an oval lawn; to the south walled gardens. To the north, the windows of the house looked over Great Oar pasture. This was how it was in 1724 when Henry Hoare died. These sur-roundings were completely changed during the next seventy-five years, particularly by Henry Hoare II, who made the lake and built the temples and other features round it between 1744 and 1770. In order to put this transformation in its context it is necessary to understand the background.

The English Landscape Movement

During the eighteenth century changes in the appearance of the landscape were greatly accelerated. Enclosure apart, 'improved' land became more valuable if trees were

6

planted, as wood was the chief raw material for the technology. To practical considerations, aesthetic and symbolic overtones were added which have their roots in Renaissance thought, two important components of which were a veneration for antiquity and a concept of Nature as an orderly system subject to laws imposed by a supreme intelligence. The primary bodies of which the universe was composed were conceived of as building materials put together in certain proportions. In terms of the human body one side corresponds to the other, and each part is related proportionally. A man with one foot bigger than the other is deformed or 'unnatural'. In this sense the Palladian style of architecture is 'natural', being constructed on the principle of symmetry about a central axis; each part relating to the other in a system of harmonic proportion. This architectural principle of regularity and balance was the ideal applied to the design of gardens in the seventeenth and early eighteenth centuries, although principles are modified by circumstances, and many gardens were irregular by reason of the conditions on the site. It was relatively easy to make a rectangular design in small walled gardens adjoining the house; beyond this, in big houses such as Stourton Manor, stretched the park, a large enclosure for deer and other animals preserved for hunting. During the seventeenth century in France, park and garden were merged in huge compositions based on the extended axis of the house, with avenues and vistas to the horizon. At Versailles, the most famous garden in Europe, the architecture of terraces and regular parterres in which the palace was set gradually gave way to trees and fields. This was indeed a 'landscape garden', a landscape controlled by art. These European gardens were admired by travellers like Addison, who wrote in 1712 that the gardens of France and Italy, where a large extent of ground was 'covered over with an agreeable mixture of garden and forest', were much more 'entertaining to the fancy' than the 'neatness and elegancy' of English gardens. However, the big French gardens were very expensive to make and maintain; it might be 'unprofitable to private persons, to alienate so much ground from pasturage and the plow. But why may not a whole estate be thrown into a kind of garden by frequent plantations that may turn as much to the profit as the pleasure of the owner?' 'Fields of corn make a pleasant prospect, and if the walks were a little taken care of that lie between them, if the natural embroidery of the meadows were helped and improved by some small additions of art. . . . a man might make a pretty landskip of his own possessions.'

Addison's words were widely read and heeded; and they sum up the spirit which, interpreted in a variety of ways, inspired the English landscape movement. The use of the ha-ha, or sunk fence, removed any visual barrier between the garden and the surrounding countryside and park, and at the same time kept the cattle and other livestock away from the house. Eventually, in the second half of the eighteenth century, Lancelot ('Capability') Brown abolished the garden altogether, setting the house directly in the park. The transition from architectural garden to Brown's idealized nature was not sudden; although once the fashion gained momentum the old gardens with their straight avenues and vistas, water confined in regular basins and canals, were rapidly transformed. The reasons were complex, and have been discussed at length by garden historians (see recommended reading), who have also tended to oversimplify the causes. Among these was the expense of constructing and maintaining stone terraces, fountains and elaborate parterres with complicated arabesque designs in box against a background of coloured earth. Even in France at the beginning of the century there was an increasing tendency to use grass in these, and to make terraces of sloping turf. When in the early 1730s William Kent (1685–1748) started to design by eye (like a painter) rather than with 'level and line' (like a surveyor), he introduced a method by which owners could dispense with a professional and do the landscaping themselves, deciding to plant here, and open up a view there, as the spirit moved them. In the mid eighteenth century before Brown started his career, many of the most celebrated landscape gardens were made in this way, by amateurs; Painshill in Surrey, Hagley in Worcestershire, the poet Shenstone's Leasowes near Halesowen, and Stourhead were all begun in the early 1740s.

But the professional continued to be employed for the design of buildings and other architectural features which proliferated in these early gardens (obelisks, temples, bridges, grottos). Whereas in the French garden the architecture was part of the structural design or closely related to it, the architectural features in early English landscape gardens were isolated incidents, either distributed widely in the landscape (Castle Howard) or marking stages in a circuit walk (Stowe, Rousham, Stourhead). Their purpose, as much as anything, was to give character to the scene by the associations they evoked, a tradition that goes back at least to the Italian humanist

Stowe from the Brick Temple, 1739, engraving Baron after Rigaud

Stowe, view from Captain Greville's Monument, 1753, engraving Bickham after Chatelain

Leone Battista Alberti (1401–1472). The first English translation of Alberti's *Ten Books of Architecture* was published in 1726. When building a country house he recommends sites with features of striking natural interest, such as 'grottoes, caverns and springs'. 'Nor should there be wanting in the prospect remains of Antiquity, on which we cannot turn our eyes without considering the various revolution of men and things, and being filled with wonder and admiration.' 'There should be Columns, Pyramids, Obelisks and other memorials to remind us of great men. The greatest ornaments are lofty towers placed in proper situations . . . and where there are a good number of them strewn up and down the country they afford a most beautiful prospect.'

The most potent source of this cult of antiquity was Italy. The European mind fed on the past grandeur of Rome, whose buildings were a model of what architecture should be, and whose literature was the foundation of a polite education: as Henry Hoare II put it, 'the pursuit of that knowledge which distinguishes only the Gentleman from the Vulgar', and without which 'the most envied height of fortune will not be enjoyed'. Nostalgia was reinforced by travel; countless Englishmen saw for themselves the places they had read about, the Roman campagna strewn with antique remains. These were represented in engravings and paintings of the kind which hang in various places in the house at Stourhead. Among the most admired were those of Claude Lorrain, Nicolas Poussin and his brother-in-law, Gaspar Dughet (who also took the name of Poussin). It is often said that these paintings inspired the English

9

R. Wilson disegnò — *Veduta del Tempio, e Fiume del Clitunno nello stato presente* — *Giuseppe Vasi intagliò*

Temple of Clitumnus, Vasi after Richard Wilson

landscape gardens; but this view has to be very considerably qualified, since, although there may be parallels, a painting cannot be *imitated* in a landscape. William Kent brought the eye of a painter to the design of gardens, but his interest was chiefly in creating a setting for his buildings, or modifying existing landscapes to the best effect, to create a variety of scenes. His style was varied and by no means always classical. Indeed the many varied ways in which antiquity is interpreted in these pre-Brown landscape gardens depends more on the whim of the owners and 'the genius of the place' than to pictorial reference. At Castle Howard it is the Howards themselves who are celebrated in the huge mausoleum. At Stowe, probably the prototype and most influential garden of its time, antiquity served the political ends of Lord Cobham and his friends, Kent's Temple of Ancient Virtue pointing the moral to contemporaries; Shenstone's Leasowes has a circuit walk with urns and seats which are memorials to friendship. Stourhead is dedicated to the pagan deities of rivers and springs; and to heroes – Aeneas, Hercules and King Alfred.

In one respect the group of gardens originating between 1730 and 1750 differed radically from the classical French gardens of Le Nôtre and Brown's landscaping, which have this in common, that they are both related to the house, either to display the architecture or to be seen from the windows. But the Grecian Valley and the Elysian Fields at Stowe, the Vale of Venus at Rousham and the journey round the lake at Stourhead are self-contained worlds, to which the owner could escape and indulge his fancy. Whatever the prototypes, in imagination they could represent anything he wished. This is quite evident when we read Henry Hoare's letters on the subject. Often they were combined with a circuit walk with stages marked by buildings having multiple functions. They are, for instance, objects forming the focal point in some living picture; at the same time they invite movement; we see them and we want to get to them. Having done so they are resting places where we can pause and contemplate what is before us; in fact many have their origins in the garden casinos of Italy away from the summer heat of Rome. Of course, in England, escape from the heat is not a problem; rather it is a question of somewhere to shelter from the rain. Lastly, the features have a symbolic meaning, or an association intended to evoke a particular response, often reinforced by an inscription with literary associations.

As regards planting, a clear distinction once existed between 'park' and 'garden'. A garden, traditionally speaking, was an enclosure for cultivating plants, with subdivisions: flower garden, vegetable garden, herb garden. The park was an area for preserving game: deer, boar or other animals. Intermediate between park and garden was a semi-wild area planted with trees and shrubs called a 'wilderness', an extended garden walk, sometimes opening out into a private retreat with some special feature: a lawn, a seat, water in various forms. The classic French example is Versailles, where the *bosquets* are contained within the regular architectural framework of the main walks and rides, which extend to embrace the landscape. The English inclined to make their *bosquets* irregular, with winding paths; and eventually to abolish the architectural framework altogether, and extend the walks, with flowers and flowering shrubs, into the park and among the pastures. This is what happened at Stourhead. One thing is evident to those who visit it, and that is that a path of great variety and interest has been contrived in a relatively small area, at different levels, now open, now enclosed; views inward to the lake and outward up Six Wells Bottom; and if you start where you should do from the lawn by the house, each feature is only gradually revealed, lost and found, until crossing the Zeals road by the rockwork bridge and climbing to Apollo's temple the whole lies open before you; as Horace Walpole said, 'one of the most picturesque scenes in the world'. There was also an outer circuit of a more pastoral character leading to Alfred's Tower and back by the Convent in the woods, emerging at the road below the dam. The essential eighteenth-century framework has remained the same, although the planting and some of the detail has changed. Even in Henry Hoare's day this was happening; and successive owners have imposed their own ideas of gardening. If you stand at the conclusion of the walk, near what may be called the entrance or the exit, depending on which way you have come, you will see coniferous trees planted in the mid nineteenth century, flowering shrubs in this century, a medieval cross, a bridge, a classical temple reflected in a lake.

The Making of Stourhead

Henry Hoare II (1705–1785) is known in the family as 'the Magnificent', which distinguishes him from all the other Henry Hoares, and suggests the lifestyle and ambition which made Stourhead, in its way, a place not to be surpassed. He was only nineteen when he succeeded to the banking business on his father's death; and at the age of twenty-one he married Ann, elder daughter of Lord Masham and of Abigail, Queen Anne's favourite. The big equestrian portrait in the hall dates from this time. Ann died in childbirth; and just over a year later he married Susan, daughter and heiress of Stephen Colt of Clapham. In early manhood he divided his time between residence over the bank in Fleet Street and a house his father had acquired at Quarley in Hampshire, where he hunted and drank with other fashionable young men, until (as he told his grandson) he found that the 'gay and dissolute style of life' was affecting his health. In 1734 he bought Wilbury House near Newton Tony in Wiltshire, from his uncle, William Benson, who had built it in the Palladian style of Inigo Jones, showing 'a particular regard to the noblest manner of architecture in this beautiful and regular design'. No doubt Benson's cultural influence was decisive for Stourhead, both in introducing his nephew to Virgil (so often referred to in the garden), and probably to artists like John Wootton, Michael Rysbrack, and Henry Flitcroft, whom Henry Hoare consistently employed up to their deaths. But as a banker he was at the centre of things. Landowners needed money for their improvements, and they borrowed it from Hoare's Bank. Names of the leaders of architectural fashion, Carlisle and Burlington, head the bank's ledgers; the more these noblemen 'improved', the more they borrowed and the more the interest mounted. Whereas the gardening passion nearly ruined many (like Charles Hamilton of Painshill), it brought only profit for Henry Hoare.

In March 1738 he went abroad for three years, mainly to Italy, returning in September 1741, when his mother died. He had not lived at Stourhead, which was left to her during her lifetime; but he probably assisted her in managing the estate. There is no direct evidence for landscaping the grounds before 1744; but in June 1757 an article by Jonas Hanway in the *London Chronicle*, describing a visit to Stourhead, referred to the Fir Walk on the hillside south-west of the house:

On the brow of the hill is a walk of considerable extent, of the softest mossy turf, bordered on each side by stately Scotch Firs of Mr. Hoare's own planting, about twenty-four years since; these, as well as the wood behind them, are rather too thickset. This noble broad Walk is terminated by an Obelisk 120 feet in height, built on the highest ground; it has a Mythra, or Sun of six feet diameter, in gilded copper at the top. This obelisk is divided from the garden by an Ha-Ha, but the view of the sheep feeding at the foot of it, has a delightful effect as if there were no such separation.

This would mean that the Walk was made about 1733; and we may assume that by that time the pleasure garden had been extended, and the walled garden shown on an estate map of 1722 turned into a lawn, lined by 'rows of beeches'. The Obelisk was not built until 1746. This first extension of the garden in a walk round Great Oar meadow, from which it was separated by a ha-ha, suggested the future development; for we may imagine that looking down on the two large ponds in the valley, and the rather bare landscape which was then before him, set Henry Hoare's mind to work as to how it could be improved. From his letters we know it is the way that his mind worked subsequently; *con spirito* (as the spirit moved him) was how Colt Hoare, his grandson, put it.

The Pattern of Perfection

It was not until after his wife died in 1743, leaving him with a son of thirteen and two daughters of eleven and six, that he decided seriously to build and plant, beginning with the little Temple of Flora (then called the Temple of Ceres), overlooking a rectangular basin near the village and a spring called Paradise Well. Henry Flitcroft, who until his death in 1769 advised Henry Hoare on all his building, was the architect. He was a protégé of Lord Burlington and hence a close associate of William Kent, whom he succeeded as Master Mason and Deputy Surveyor in the Office of Works, becoming Comptroller in 1758.

The letters Flitcroft wrote in 1744 are the first direct pieces of evidence concerning Henry Hoare's plan for the gardens. They are supported by the meticulous accounts kept by Henry himself in his personal ledgers. The first two letters refer to 'the Venetian Seat' and 'the Circular open Temple of the Ionick Order'. The first is probably the seat illustrated by the Swedish artist, F.M.Piper, in 1799, which stood at the northeast end of the terrace, where the path begins to descend. Of the second there is no other record or trace; it may have been an early design for a temple on the site of the Pantheon, about which Henry Hoare changed his mind. Flitcroft's second letter concludes: 'My next shall bring you sections of the proper moulding for this building, and after that the Temple of Ceres, with the Rocky Arch in which I propose to place the River God, and a sketch of how I conceive the head [1] of the lake should be formed. Twill make a most agreeable scene, with the solemn shade about it and the variety of other agreeable circumstances.' The project was an enormous undertaking. The size of the dam apart, it was not just a matter of building it and letting the water find its own level; the borders of the lake were constructed, with shelving stones some

[1] i.e. dam. *cf Shorter OED*: 'Head II. 10. A body of water kept at a height for supplying a mill . . . sometimes the bank or dam by which such water is kept up.' See also Pocock's remark under DAM p.53.

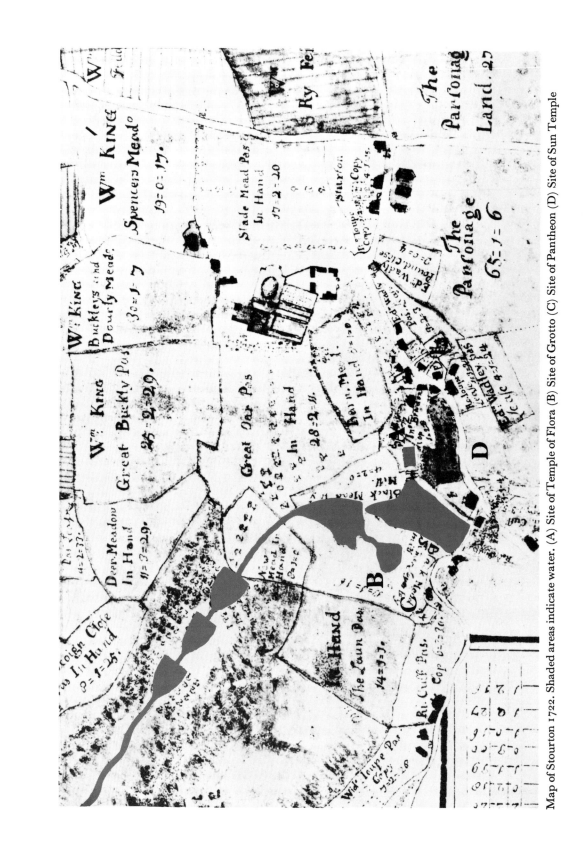

Map of Stourton 1722. Shaded areas indicate water. (A) Site of Temple of Flora (B) Site of Grotto (C) Site of Pantheon (D) Site of Sun Temple

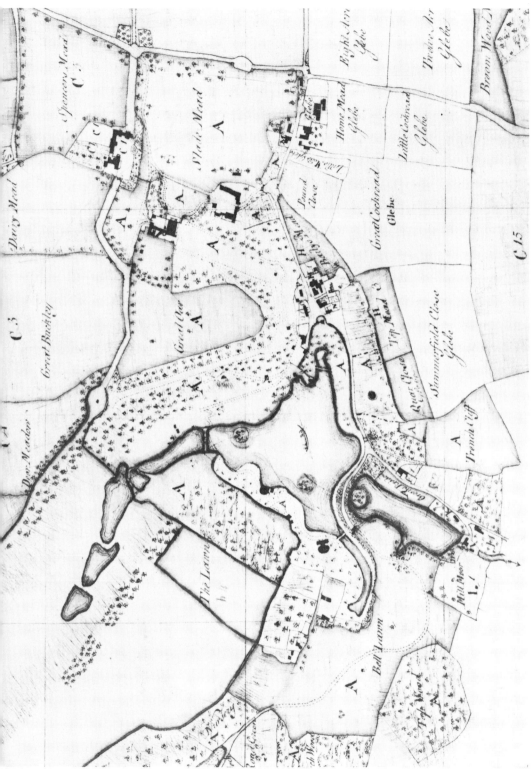

Plan of the Grounds on Henry Hoare's death in 1785

(*Above*) Temple of Flora, C.W. Bampfylde, 1753

(*Right*) Temple on the Terrace, F.M. Piper, 1779

yards into the water. The various features round it had to be made before the water was allowed to rise. The work was done continuously in an anti-clockwise sequence, as the payments to the builders show; at first to Nathaniel Ireson, who had been established in Stourton since 1720, and who had built the house; and then from 1745 to William Privet of Chilmark near Tisbury in Wiltshire. He received payments for 'the temple' (Flora) in 1745–6; 'the Obelisk' 1747–50; 'the bridge and other work' 1749–50. This was the wooden bridge of one arch after Palladio, which was to carry the path to the Grotto over the north arm of the lake. Privet's detailed account for the Grotto was made out in 1748. It was a symmetrical building, whose original pedimented entrance is buried in the dark serpentine passage added in 1776.

There was a pause in the work of building after 1750, if we are to judge by Henry Hoare's accounts. There are no payments to Privet in 1751; and it is not until 1753 that records of the building of the Pantheon begin. There were very good reasons for this lull in operations. The death of his only surviving son at Naples in 1751, at the age of twenty-one, was a great blow. As he wrote to his brother, 'I have been taught by our Holy Religion, and by former visitations, tryals and afflictions to submit myself before the throne of God who . . . still supports me under a grief I never expected or wished to have survived.' Left without an heir he may well have felt discouraged from immediate thoughts of adorning Stourhead; but he was also planning to build the house designed by Flitcroft overlooking Clapham Common, to which he ultimately retired. In 1753 his elder daughter, Susanna, was married to Lord Dungarvan, son of John Boyle, Earl of Orrery. Meanwhile he was planning the marriage of his younger daughter Anne (called 'Nanny') to Richard Hoare, son of his only brother. It was during their engagement that he wrote the letters to his nephew which are so characteristic of the man, his philosophy and style, sprinkled with phrases from his varied reading, which included Milton, Pope and Akenside, Virgil and Ovid. 'Whether at pleasure or business let us be in earnest,' he wrote 'and ever active to be outdone or exceeded by none, that is the way to thrive.' 'I hear you have been at Stourhead without the Dame, and so saw undelighted all delight tho' you trod the enchanting paths of Paradise . . . What is there in creation . . . those are the fruits of industry and application to business and shows what great things may be done by it, the envy of the indolent who have no claim to temples, grottos, bridges, rocks, exotic pines and ice in summer. When those are won by the industrious, they have the best claim to them provided their foundations is laid by the hand of prudence and supported by perseverance in well-doing and constant cautious watchfulness over the main chance. Without it proud Versailles thy glory falls and Nero's terrasses desert their walls, so you could not go on your Via Charmgiana, it is a pattern of perfection.'

The Classical Heroes

Nanny and Richard were married in March 1756, and it was in the years leading up to this event that the Pantheon was built. Whether or not it was part of the original concept, it could be argued that it is the most important visual component of the whole design. In the Temple of Flora Henry Hoare was honouring the sources of the river in the pagan manner, with a temple such as the younger Pliny had described at Clitumnus. Its site, like that of the Grotto, was determined by the springs. The siting of the Pantheon is a matter of pictorial effect. Looking from the hillside near the house it is a substantial object in the middle distance. It was first called the Temple of Hercules and was clearly intended to house Michael Rysbrack's statue of the hero, which Henry had commissioned in 1747. Hercules was one of the deities associated with gardens in Roman times; and even earlier with Greek mystery cults and their sacred gardens. In the Renaissance, Hercules was a great moral hero. The myth of how he took the golden apples from the garden of the Hesperides was interpreted as the mastery of the three vices: Anger, Avarice and Sensual Pleasure. Hercules at the cross-roads, choosing between Pleasure and Virtue, was a favourite allegory; and Henry Hoare owned a painting of the subject by Nicolas Poussin, which now hangs in the Picture Gallery. At the same time the Pantheon was held up as a model by Renaissance pattern books. In the English translation of Serlio's *Book of Architecture* (1611) we read: 'Among all the ancient building to be seene in Rome, I am of opinion, that the Pantheon (for one piece of worke alone) is the fayrest, wholest, and best to be understood.' The most admired of Roman buildings, dedicated to the greatest hero and set in ideal nature was, as Henry Hoare put it, 'a pattern of perfection'.

View from the Mount of Diana, anonymous engraving, c.1765–70

Of course this is only part of the iconography of the garden, although a very important one. The statues, inscriptions and attributions of the various buildings constitute a body of reference to various sources. The lines from Pope on the pavement in the Grotto acknowledge his inspiration. The statue of the nymph derives from a statue in the Belvedere Garden of the Vatican, of which many copies were made, the earliest being for François I at Fontainebleau (now in the Louvre). Two giant antique figures of *Tiber* and *Nile*, also in the Vatican garden, gave rise to numerous reclining River Gods, of which Henry Hoare bought a debased descendant from Thomas Manning in 1743. It was placed in the 'rocky arch' which Flitcroft designed for him over Paradise Well below the Temple of Flora. Most of Henry Hoare's garden statues came from John Cheere, who provided casts in lead and plaster as garden furniture. Many of them were after originals at Versailles, which had the largest and most celebrated programme of garden statuary in Europe.

There is not strictly speaking a sculpture programme at Stourhead; but there is a theme, which is announced in the inscriptions on the original entrance to the Grotto, buried in later additions, and over the door of the Temple of Flora. Both are from the *Aeneid*, Virgil's epic about the founding of Rome. The first, as is suitable for a nymphaeum, associates the Grotto with the cave of the nymphs where Aeneas lands in North Africa on his flight from Troy; the second, 'Procul, O procul este profani' ('Begone, you who are uninitiated! Begone!') is spoken by the Cumaean Sybil before leading Aeneas into the underworld where the future history of Rome will be revealed to him. This suggests that at some time the path to the Pantheon was associated with Aeneas's journey. There are further clues, in that Henry Hoare made a direct analogy in one of his letters to his daughter. 'I have made the passage up from the Sousterrain serpentine and will make it easier of access facilis descensus Averno.' 'Light is the descent into Avernus,' says the Sybil, 'but to recall thy step and issue to the upper air, there is the toil and there the task.' And this is not pure conjecture; another statue of a River God was bought from Cheere in 1751 and placed in the cave over the spring outside the Grotto. The prototype for this statue is not classical but is derived from an etching by Salvator Rosa, one of a series of studies called *The Dream of Aeneas*. The story is that Aeneas, having landed in Italy with his band of Trojan survivors, is in need of allies to help him in his war against Latium. 'Tossed in a heaving tide of anxieties', he sinks down on to the river bank and sleeps. 'And there appeared to him the God of the place, old Tiber himself, who arose from his pleasant stream amid his poplar leaves. A fine linen clothed him in grey raiment, and shady reeds covered his hair.' He tells Aeneas 'here is your home assured and here for the Gods of Home is their sure place'. He prophesies victory and tells Aeneas to seek out the Arcadians as allies. On waking, Aeneas, in gratitude to the river nymphs and Father Tiber, swears that 'whatever spring may fill the pools which are your home, and wherever you yourself emerge in grandeur from the soil, always shall you be celebrated by me . . .' Cheere's figure shows Tiber (or Stour if you like) exactly as

Aeneas at Delos, Claude Lorrain, National Gallery, London

Virgil describes him. He points the way to the Pantheon, just as in the *Aeneid*, following Tiber's advice, Aeneas seeks out the Arcadian king and finds him engaged in rites at an altar dedicated to the worship of Hercules.

There is one other piece of evidence which, in view of the rest, seems more than a coincidence. There is a picture by Claude Lorrain in the National Gallery called *Coast View of Delos with Aeneas* which shows the Pantheon, bridge and Doric portico bearing a curious resemblance to the way in which similar buildings are related to the garden at Stourhead. It represents an episode in Aeneas's journey, before his arrival in Italy. Aeneas, his father Anchises and his son Ascanius are standing on the terrace at Delos, the birthplace of Apollo and Diana, with Anius the priest. Aeneas prays, 'Apollo, grant us a home of our own. We are weary. Give us a walled city which shall endure and a lineage of our blood.' In 1751 Aeneas's prayer must have had a poignant relevance for Henry Hoare. The previous year his son had written from Aix concerning pictures by Claude which he had been asked to buy. Had Henry Hoare at some time seen *Coast View of Delos with Aeneas*? He had a copy of a similar painting (now in the Picture Gallery) but he was never able to possess an original. Like Aeneas, he was establishing his family in a place. This is not to say that the features were planned with an allegorical intention; but at some time between 1744 and 1751 the association with the *Aeneid* was made. Henry Hoare was a master of the 'pleasures of the imagination'; he took lessons from what he read and his fancy found a link with what he was doing in the landscape. This is quite in accordance with what we know about certain of his subsequent building, particularly Alfred's Tower.

A Charming Gaspar Picture

By 1757 the Pantheon was built, the dam complete, and the lake had assumed more or less the form we see today. The path from the terrace zig-zagged down the hill crossing the north arm of the lake by a wooden bridge of one arch. As Hanway wrote in June that year, 'In this delicious abode are no Chinese works, no monsters of imagination, no deviations from nature, under the fond notions of fashion or taste; all is grand, or simple, or a beautiful mixture of both.' When Horace Walpole saw it in 1762 he had little to add to the picture, beyond an account of the furniture of the Pantheon. 'Behind the Hercules', he noted, 'is a large grate of brass to admit heat from a stove, and looking like a grate for Nuns in a catholic chapel.' And on the slopes near the village (between the present entrance and the Temple of Flora) 'a green-house of false Gothick'. There was a statue of Apollo on a mount at the end of the lawn south of the house, from where a path led to the terrace. A visitor in 1766 wrote that 'the first object that strikes you is a Chinese Pavilion', from where 'you suddenly

Panorama of east side of lake (detail), C.W. Bampfylde Victoria and Albert Museum

(*Above*) Bridge and
Obelisk, C.W. Bampfylde

(*Right*) Gothic greenhouse,
detail, from panorama of
east side of lake
C.W. Bampfylde

View from Chinese Umbrella, F.M. Piper, 1779

have a fine view of the lake and temple'. The situation suits the picture by the Swedish artist F.M. Piper of a 'Chinese Umbrella'. On the other hand, Piper's plan shows a rectangular structure called a 'Chinese Alcove' where the path changes direction down the hill, so that in the absence of more evidence the interpretation must remain open.

Meanwhile Henry Hoare was affected by another personal tragedy. 'Nanny', whose first child had died in infancy, gave birth to a second, Richard Colt Hoare, in December 1758. She died the following May, not long before her twenty-second birthday. Susanna's husband, Lord Dungarvan, also died, leaving a daughter, Henrietta. Susanna was married again in 1761, to Lord Bruce of Tottenham, later Earl of Ailesbury. The letters Henry wrote to his aristocratic son-in-law, to Susanna ('Sukey') and Henrietta ('Harriot'), confide his most personal feelings about the garden, record all that he is doing and give a vivid picture of him in later life. In the hot summer of 1764 he wrote:

We dine with the hall doors open into the staircase, which we never did before, for the door into the air would let in the heat of a firey furnace . . . A souse in that delicious bath and grot, filld with fresh magic, is Asiatick luxury, and too much for mortals, or at least for subjects. Next I ride under the spreading beeches just beyond the Obelisk where we are sure of wind and shade and a delightful view into the vale . . .

Sometime between 1760 and 1765 he made the rock bridge across the Zeals road, leading to the Temple of Apollo and presumably the underpass returning to the lake.

23

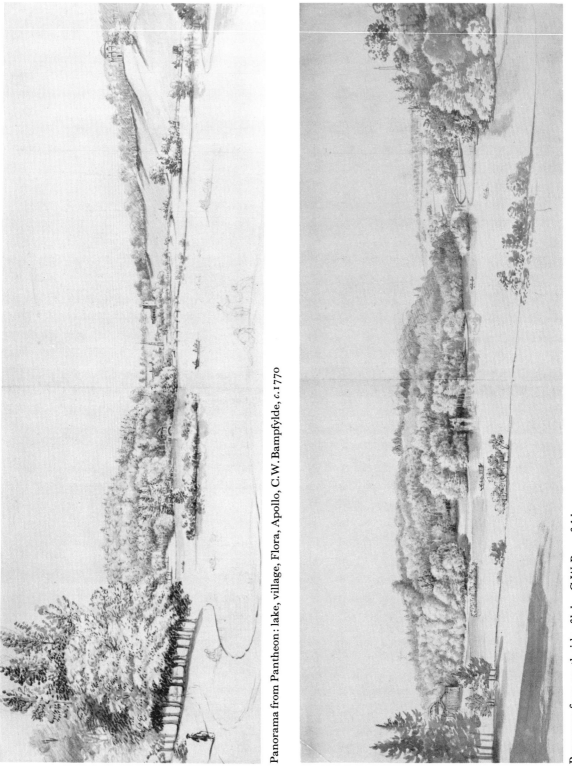

Panorama from Pantheon: lake, village, Flora, Apollo, C.W. Bampfylde, *c.*1770

Panorama from south side of lake, C.W. Bampfylde, *c.*1770

This temple was the last of the classical buildings designed by Flitcroft, after the engraving of a temple in Robert Wood's *Ruins of Balbec* of which Henry Hoare bought a copy in 1757. With its scalloped entablature the temple departed from the strict Palladian canon. The design had been anticipated by William Chambers at Kew in 1761. Below the Temple of Apollo a new scene had come into being. Standing at the Pantheon Henry Hoare looked back on the village of Stourton and its church, centuries older than the classical scene he was creating. Some owners removed villages which interfered with their improvements; but Henry Hoare wrote to Susanna in October 1762 announcing 'the Stone Bridge of 5 arches you always wished I would build at the passage into the orchard and the scheme of carrying the water up and losing out of sight towards the parish. This Bridge is now about. It is simple and plain. I took it from Palladio's bridge at Vicenza, 5 arches; and when you stand at the Pantheon the water will be seen thro the arches and it will look as if the river came down through the village and that this was the village bridge for publick use. The view of the bridge, village and church altogether will be a charm(in)g Gasp(ar)d picture at that end of the water.' Between the bridge and the church he erected the Bristol High Cross, a medieval monument he acquired in 1764. It had originally stood at a cross-roads in the city, but was removed by petition of the citizens who described it as '. . . a ruinous and superstitious Relick, which is at present a public nuisance . . .' The pieces lay neglected in a corner of the cathedral, until they were rescued by Henry Hoare with the permission of his friend the Dean. They were transported to Wiltshire in six wagons in October 1764; but it was not until December the next year that Henry Hoare wrote to Lord Bruce: 'The Cross is now in hand and there are so many pieces that we must I believe employ Harriot to put it together as she is such an adept in joyning the map of the Countys of England.' Another medieval monument from Bristol was erected over the springs in Six Wells Bottom. The rustic Convent in the woods also appears to date from about this time; and possibly the Watch Cottage, although it was hidden in the trees and had not got the later additions of seat and porch.

King Alfred

Although the Gothic taste was undergoing a revival, stimulated by Horace Walpole's example at Strawberry Hill, it had never entirely been out of fashion. It was used by Vanbrugh and Kent wherever it seemed appropriate; and at Stowe it had political significance. The British, it was held, inherited their freedom from their Saxon ancestors. 'Gothic' was 'Saxon'; there were no fine stylistic distinctions. The temple at Stowe designed by James Gibbs in the early 1740s was dedicated 'to the Liberty of our Ancestors'. In 1765 Henry Hoare's antiquarian enthusiasm was not particularly original; moreover he was no purist. While he was installing the Cross, he was also putting up a statue of Neptune in the front of the Temple of Flora. Why he did this or what it was like we do not know, for it hardly figures in later drawings, and had completely disappeared by the second decade of the nineteenth century.

The same letter which informed Susanna about the village scene continues as follows:

I have one more scheme which will crown or top all. As I was reading Voltaire's *L'Histoire Générale* lately, in his character of Alfred the Great he says, Je ne sai s'il y a jamais eu sur la terre un homme plus digne des respects de la posterité qu'Alfred le Grand, qui rendit ces services à sa patrie. Out of gratitude to him I propose . . . to erect a Tower on Kingsettle Hill where he set up his standard after he came from his concealment in the Isle of Athelney near Taunton, and the Earl of Devon had worsted the Danes . . . I intend to build it on the plan of Sn Marks Tower at Venice, 100 foot to the room which the staircase will lead to and 4 arches to look out in the 4 sides to the prospect allround.

Alfred had a political significance. Thirty years earlier his bust had appeared in the Temple of British Worthies at Stowe; for just as 'Gothic' was a symbol of British liberty, so Alfred symbolized the ideal of a British king, as opposed to the first two Hanoverians who were predominantly German, with a strong inclination to put Hanoverian before British interests. For this reason George II had been a strong influence in the continuation of war against France in Europe, which had been almost continuous for twenty years. Alfred's Tower celebrated both peace and the accession of George III. It was completed in 1772, ironically on the eve of the next

King Alfred, Rysbrack
(*Photo, K.Woodbridge*)

disastrous war. The wording of the inscription was carefully discussed. Henry's first draft included the words, 'Erected, Anno Dom: 1762 in the 3rd Glorious Year of the Reign of our truely British King George the 3rd'.

The final version, with slight modification, was Lord Bruce's. It omits a reference to King George, referring to Alfred as:

The Father of his people
The Founder of the English Monarchy and Liberty.

Alfred is not a complete break with the earlier hero as he at first seems. According to the twelfth-century chronicle of Geoffrey of Monmouth, Aeneas, through his grandson Brutus the Trojan, was an ancestor of the British race. Moreover the character of Alfred as interpreted by Henry Hoare and his contemporaries has affinities with Numa, the philosopher king of Rome, who got his wisdom from the nymph Egeria who lived in a cave.

The Hermit

William Hoare, the portrait painter, was a frequent visitor to Stourhead. He was no relation, but his daughter married one of Henry's nephews. Another regular visitor was Copplestone Warre Bampfylde, amateur painter, architect and landscape enthusiast, who made many drawings of Stourhead. In the grounds of his house at Hestercombe, near Taunton, he had constructed an ingenious cascade, falling from a height among rocks; and in 1765, with the help of William Hoare, he devised the cascade at Stourhead which falls into the lake below the dam. Charles Hamilton, creator of a famous landscape garden at Painshill, Surrey, also gave advice. There was a Turkish Tent of painted canvas at Stourhead, similar to the one at Painshill. It stood on a level below the terrace with a view of the lake and the Pantheon. In November 1771, Henry wrote to his grand-daughter, Harriot:

I am building a Hermitage above the Rock and when you are about a quarter part up the walk from the Rock to the Temple of Apollo you turn short to the right and so zig-zag up to it and thence go under the trees to the Temple of Apollo as Mr Hamilton advised. And we stop or plant up in clumps the old walk up the hill to that temple. It is to be lined inside and out with old gouty knobbly oakes, the bark on, which Mr. Groves and my neighbours are so kind to give me; and Mr. Chapman a clergyman showed me one yesterday called Judge Wyndham's Seat which I take to be of the year of our Lord one thousand, and I am not quite sure that it is not Anti Diluvian. I believe I shall put in to be myself the hermit.

The Hermitage or Druid's Cell has long since disappeared. The arched recess on the right of the path to the Temple of Apollo is all that remains of it.

At the age of seventy Henry Hoare was still busy adding new touches to his creation. Besides the more sophisticated travellers, 'crowds of country people' now visited the garden; but among Henry's chief pleasures was the interest of his daughter and her children. It was the latter who could probably more nearly enter into the spirit of the place and share his own childlike enthusiasms. 'I am upon the entrance to the Grotto to get it finished before you come,' he told Susanna in May 1776. 'It is a spot of such romantick pleasure as to strike everybody and nothing here ever delighted me so much. The dear Charles [1] has shook off his cold and trudges down to Mary Faugoin's [2] with his wagon twice a day, and has found the easy path to and from it.' Later in the month he wrote to Lord Bruce, 'Thank God they are all fine and well, and now make nothing of walking round the gardens; and I mounted the Tower Thursday with the dear children. The Temple of the Nymph is all enchantment to them, and the Cross new painted fills them with rapture.'

As the news of war grew worse, however, Henry Hoare became increasingly pessimistic. In 1779, French and Spanish ships lay unopposed off Plymouth and all England expected an invasion. Bampfylde, who had been sketching in North Devon, wrote that the combined fleets had been seen off the Lizard. 'The accounts are so various,' wrote Henry, 'we are tossed in a sea of troubles and uncertainty, and kept in hot water; and I pray God to deliver us . . . I am afraid to enquire after the news, and wish to think of politics and partys no more.'

In 1780 there were seven days of rioting in London, particularly violent in the Fleet Street area. Henry had fears for the future of his business, and was determined that in the case of a disaster the creditors should not lay hands on Stourhead. He therefore determined to leave his west country property to his grandson, Richard Colt Hoare, son of Nanny and his nephew Richard, on condition that he gave up all connection with the bank. On Colt's marriage he retired, as he had said, to Clapham where, having outlived Susanna, his last surviving child, he died in September 1785.

1. Charles Bruce, 1st Marquis of Ailesbury.
2. Wife of Francis Faugoin, Henry Hoare's steward.

Transformations: 1791–1946

Sir Richard Colt Hoare (1758-1838), 2nd Baronet

The broad structure of Henry Hoare's landscape has been preserved by subsequent owners. Alterations in the grounds immediately surrounding the house were made by Sir Richard Colt Hoare, who also laid down gravel paths, establishing a pattern which has persisted to the present day. Otherwise the most significant changes have been in the character of the planting, as an increasing number of exotic trees and shrubs became available. Colt Hoare bridged the eighteenth and nineteenth centuries; he had his roots in the classical culture of his grandfather's generation, but he also looked forward to high Victorian fashion for exotic planting. Brought up with a family of half brothers and sisters in his father's house at Barn Elms, 'a delightful and extensive villa on the banks of the Thames' between Putney and Mortlake, he was also strongly influenced by his grandfather, 'tall and comely in person, elegant in his manners and address and well versed in polite literature'. As a schoolboy his summer holidays were spent at Stourhead, where he saw the building of the Sun Temple, the arrival of the Cross and the rise of Alfred's Tower. But he had none of Henry Hoare's ebullience. Excluded from the bank, his conscientious and industrious disposition found satisfaction in scholarship; and whereas Henry Hoare imposed a classical vision on the Wiltshire countryside, Colt Hoare recorded its past, most notably in the various

Prehistoric earthworks on Whitesheet Down. (*Aerial photo, J.E. Hancock*)

29

volumes of his histories of *Ancient* and *Modern Wiltshire*. A circumstance which un-doubtedly contributed to this development was the death in 1785 of his wife, Hester Lyttelton, shortly after their marriage. Not only was Stourhead without any female influence for the next fifty years, but Colt Hoare felt the loss of this lively, cultivated, highly strung girl so deeply that, except for a brief period in 1787, he remained abroad for six years, leaving his estates in charge of his steward.

His temperament and education were eminently suited to the experience of Italy, where (as he later wrote) 'every scene bears a classic character, and every district acquires double interest from the recollections it calls forth'. Scenes from the *Aeneid*, about which he must often have heard at Stourhead, were brought to life. Moreover his observation had been sharpened by lessons in watercolour painting from John 'Warwick' Smith, and for the first part of his life he was a prolific if uninspired draughtsman. When Turner visited Stourhead about 1800 he took Colt Hoare's own drawing of Lake Avernus and painted *Lake Avernus with Aeneas and the Cumean Sibyl*, which hung in the Cabinet Room at Stourhead until it was sold by the 5th Baronet in 1883. When Colt Hoare returned to England in July 1791, driven home by events which made residence abroad difficult and dangerous, he was a man of substance. On his father's death in 1787 he had become Sir Richard Colt Hoare, 2nd Baronet. He owned 11,000 acres, most of them adjoining Stourton and Gaspar, with outlying estates in Wiltshire, Somerset and Dorset. His gross annual rental was between £9,000 and £10,000, which put him high in the group of the three hundred wealthy men immediately below the great landed nobility. Stourhead had remained virtually as his grandfather had left it; but now that the lines of his personality were set, he turned to making a place conformable with his own tastes and way of life. The addi-

View of lake with bridge, Temple of Apollo, Pantheon, S.H. Grimm, 1790, British Museum

tion of the Library and Picture Gallery pavilions to the house completely changed its appearance from the front. The approach drive was resited in its present position while a new drive was made from the north, and the park extended on that side. The library wing destroyed the symmetry of Campbell's south façade, so that the regular lawn flanked by lines of beeches, with the statue of Apollo marking the axis on that side, lost its point. By cutting down some of the beeches to break the regularity, and by planting other trees, Colt Hoare sought to adapt the grounds to the less formal style then fashionable.

Elsewhere, while generally applauding what Henry Hoare had done, he disapproved of 'nature overcrowded with buildings', particularly if these were not in harmony with one another. His object, he wrote, was to render the design of the gardens as chaste and correct as possible, and to give them the character of an Italian villa. Henry Hoare, as we have seen, saw no objection to including buildings of different styles. On Piper's plan of 1779 a number of these are shown among the trees on the hillside nearest the house. The Turkish Tent, which was of painted canvas, standing on a platform below the Fir Walk, had already disappeared by 1792; but Colt Hoare pulled down the Venetian Seat at the end of the terrace ('Y' on Piper's plan), moving the copy of the Borghese Vase and the two busts which it contained to the Temple of Flora. He also destroyed the 'greenhouse of false Gothic' (Piper's 'Orangery', 'F'); and a Chinese Alcove ('D' on Piper's plan), of whose appearance there is no record. The wooden Palladian bridge over the north arm of the lake, which was unsafe, was taken down in 1798 and replaced by a ferry. The remains of the Hermitage on Apollo's hill were not removed till 1814.

Colt Hoare did very little building in the region of the lake. The rock-work boat-house beyond the Temple of Flora was finished in 1794. In 1806 the cottage between the Grotto and the Pantheon was turned into a picturesque feature, with the addition of a 'Gothic' porch and seat by the architectural draughtsman John Carter, a fanatical enthusiast for ancient fabrics. Colt Hoare, in common with his generation, had an eye for the picturesque and leanings to the Gothic style. The lodges built at the approaches to the house were in a Tudor style. In the village, he pulled down cottages which obscured the view of the church and the gardens; and added Gothic-style parapets like those on the church to other houses to create a unified effect. He also changed the sign of the Inn from that of the river Stour to the Spread Eagle, his family crest.

The first gravel path, laid down in 1792, was from the village to the Temple of Flora. Another round the north arm of the lake, between Diana's Basin and the lily pond, brought a part of the park, formerly outside, into the garden. Finally the public road was fenced off, and a path was made from the stone bridge to the rock arch, by-passing the Temple of Apollo. A public entrance in the village was a convenience, but the general result was to make a walk at one level round the lake easier on the legs, but lacking the variety and dramatic impact of the approach from the house at a higher level. Moreover, as Colt himself observed, the scene from the Cross should be the final view in Henry Hoare's circuit, not the first one. Another effect of gravel paths is to invite planting on either side. The big open space between the Temple of Flora and the wooden bridge began to fill with shrubs, thus compromising the balance of tree mass and void in the broad design of the landscape. Indeed it was Colt Hoare who introduced *Rhododendron ponticum* and later *R. arboreum*, some enormous specimens of which survive. At the same time the south side of the lake, which had remained very bare, was planted with ornamental trees, and the naked turf of Apollo's hill was clothed with laurel, so that the temple seemed to float in a sea of green. The woodland was also extensively underplanted with laurel. The invasive nature of both this and *R. ponticum* overwhelmed the borders of the lake before the end of the century. In the massive planting programme he began in 1791 he reinforced the existing pattern with deciduous forest trees, particularly beech, while eliminating what he called the 'fir tribe'. Thus in 1792 he noted 'began to cut down the Fir Walk', whose points now obtruded into the silhouette of the woods from the lake.

Colt Hoare belonged to a more sophisticated generation of plantsmen than his grandfather's. He was a member of the Linnean Society and numbered among his friends A.B. Lambert, the author of *The Genus Pinus*, the second volume of which (1824) is dedicated to him. Colt Hoare was also known for his collection of geraniums

View of church, inn and cross, S.H. Grimm, 1790, British Museum

Temple of Flora from the north, F. Nicholson, *c.*1813

Stourhead, J. Constable, 1811, Fogg Art Museum, Harvard University

The lake from the cross, F. Nicholson, c. 1813

South side of lake from dam, F. Nicholson, c.1811

or hybrid pelargoniums, which were housed in a conservatory running parallel to the Library from the south-west corner of the house. Beginning in 1809 with the purchase of fifty-three species, by 1821 he had some six hundred varieties.

A complete visual record of the grounds was made by the artist Francis Nicholson between 1811 and 1813. It includes the long panorama of the lake in the ante-room to the Library; and a magnificent series of watercolours which were sold in 1883, the bulk of which are in the British Museum, although a few are in private collections. Colt Hoare also instituted *The Annals of Stourhead*, a yearly record of building, planting and other noteworthy events, which was kept from 1792 to 1860 and from 1894 to 1947. Here we read that the Gardener's House was remodelled in 1808; and that it was burnt down in 1813. Nicholson's painting of this picturesque building, with its thatched roof, neat lawn and bed of hollyhocks (see cover), must therefore have been made before then. It stood roughly on the site of the present kiosk. Among his other alterations in the grounds he enlarged the arm of the lake between the stone bridge and the village in 1814; and in 1820 he undertook a major piece of landscaping in making a piece of water of fourteen acres at Gaspar, below Turner's Paddock lake. Although in early life he spent many months of the year away from Stourhead, for the last eighteen years he was almost permanently in residence, only leaving to go to Bath for his gout and rheumatism. He died in 1838 at the age of eighty.

The lake from Six Wells Bottom, F. Nicholson, *c*.1813

Six Wells Bottom from St Peter's Pump, F. Nicholson, *c*.1813

36

View of Alfred's Tower, F. Nicholson, *c*.1813

The Convent, F. Nicholson, *c*.1813

The Victorians

For the next eighteen years Stourhead came under the good management of Colt's half brother, Henry Hugh Hoare, and his son Hugh Richard, respectively the 3rd and 4th Baronets. Both were partners in the Bank and were thus able to bring additional resources to maintaining the estates. Henry Hugh was only four years younger than Colt and had three more years to live. Moreover he already had a house and estate at Wavendon in Buckinghamshire, bought by their father. Yet he left his mark on Stourhead, chiefly by adding a portico to the house, according to Colen Campbell's original intention. The Obelisk was taken down and rebuilt with Bath stone; it was then ninety years old and possibly unsafe; and the lodge beyond it, begun by Colt Hoare, was completed. The architect was Charles Parker.

Sir Henry Hugh died at Wavendon in 1841. Hugh Richard, who was then fifty-four and a partner in the Bank, retired to Stourhead in 1845, and devoted the rest of his life to farming. His annual allowance from the business permitted the income from the farms on his estate to be put to their improvement. His monuments in the landscape were new agricultural buildings, farmhouses and cottages, with tiled roofs replacing thatch. Nearly each year new ones were added to Stourton farm: stables, wagon-houses, cattle and lambing sheds; similarly at Brewham and Kilmington, where his initials 'H.R.H.', in bold, square letters, can be seen on the cottage facing the road to Alfred's Tower. The iron hurdles fencing the park opposite the mansion date from that time. Other marks of the good farmer there undoubtedly were; new land brought under cultivation, good drainage, trim hedging. A more lasting influence is seen in the trees he planted. The commercial woodlands were stocked with spruce, larch and Scotch fir; new species of conifer added to the character of the pleasure grounds, their dark accents enriching the winter landscape. Some of these have reached huge proportions, and are among the earliest of the kind grown in England; for example, the western red cedar (*Thuja plicata*) on the left of the path before it forks to by-pass the Grotto or the coast redwood (*Sequoia sempervirens*).

Only twice in its history did son succeed to father at Stourhead. When the 4th Baronet died without issue in 1857, it passed to his nephew, Henry Ainslie Hoare, who was then thirty-three and living in Paris. He and his wife Augusta first became acquainted with Stourhead when they spent the first part of their honeymoon there in 1845 before going abroad. Sir Henry Ainslie's restless temperament found satisfaction in a varied and active social life and in politics. He was Liberal Member of Parliament for New Windsor from 1865 to 1866, and for Chelsea from 1868 to 1874. The centres of his life were London and Paris; Stourhead was chiefly a place for hunting and shooting parties in the autumn, or providing fresh vegetables for his London entertainments. Its management was in the hands of his steward, Robert Shackleton. Soon after taking possession, Sir Henry Ainslie had a new fountain erected outside his wife's window, on the lawn where she later buried all her dogs; and in the same year (1860), the oak bridge beyond the Pantheon was replaced by the present iron bridge. These are the only structural features recorded in the gardens during Sir Henry Ainslie's thirty-seven years as owner. After the first wave of enthusiasm, the *Annals* were discontinued until 1893. But whatever Stourhead may have lost to support Henry Ainslie's lifestyle in London or Paris, there is no evidence that he did not understand the economic value of good forestry and satisfied farming tenants. Each year from 1857 to 1885 Shackleton's daybooks report a regular correspondence with his employer, and frequent sessions with him during the time he was in residence.

Augusta had a firm attachment to Stourhead, which she always referred to as 'home', even though she only spent a small part of each year there. She and Sir Henry led mainly independent social lives. The happiest passages in her journals are those which talk of the times she spent at Stourhead with her four grandchildren; rides in the woods or gardens in donkey-chairs and wagonettes; picnics at the Convent or Alfred's Tower; parties in the Picture Gallery with the village children. In November 1885 after Sir Henry Ainslie contested the East Somerset seat as a Tory and lost, he decided he could no longer afford to live at Stourhead; and failing to find a tenant, he put up the shutters. Augusta later wrote in her journal, 'How little I thought I was leaving my beloved home for ever.' And on 11 June 1886 she wrote, 'Drove to my beloved Stourton. Walked round the lake which was looking lovely. Saw several people and fairly broke down when I got to the Rectory.' The house was unoccupied until 1894. While she remained in the London house at Eaton Place, the 5th Baronet

Cottages and cross, photo, 1901

Rhododendrons, late nineteenth-century photograph

Bridge and lake with newly planted conifers, late nineteenth-century photograph

spent much of his time in France. He was taken ill at Nice in March 1894; returned to England in May, and died at Eaton Place in July. He was buried at Stourton.

Sir Henry Hoare (1894-1947), 6th Baronet

Henry Hugh Arthur Hoare, who became the 6th Baronet, was then twenty-nine. He was not a stranger to Stourhead, for he had taken over the management of the woodlands in 1891, and Sir Henry Ainslie's solicitors had written in February 1894 giving his consent 'to Topwood being planted for scenic effect not for profit'. While the house was renovated and furniture from Wavendon moved into it, the 6th Baronet and his wife lived in the agent's house opposite the church (then called 'The Cottage', now the National Trust Regional Office). After seven years' neglect the pleasure grounds were overgrown with laurel and rhododendron; the Bristol Cross was in imminent danger of falling down; the Grotto was entirely overgrown by laurel, which had penetrated the stonework, and the roof threatened to collapse. Between 1894 and 1900 all the buildings were repaired and the Watch Cottage restored and furnished as a sitting room; although it was not until 1907–08 that it was re-roofed with stone tiles from an old cottage in West Knoyle. At the same time he began the task of clearing and replanting, introducing new varieties of ornamental tree and shrub. At that point a disaster happened. In 1902 the centre block of the house was gutted by fire. While it was being rebuilt Sir Henry and his family had to return to 'The Cottage'.

Sir Henry lived the conventional life of a country gentleman at Stourhead longer than any of his predecessors. He had no connection with Hoare's Bank. Although as a director of Lloyds Bank he went regularly to London for meetings, his main interests were in country matters, particularly horses, on which he was an expert and noted for his breed of percherons, a horse of French origin combining strength with speed. He gave a new character to the gardens in which he took a particular pride. Some parts he transformed; thus in 1895–6 'a new hatch was put into Diana's Basin', in the north-west corner, and it was 'reconverted to a pond'. Between the wars many new flowering shrubs were added, especially varieties of rhododendron replacing large areas of what he called 'the common sort', which were grubbed out. In his last years he suffered badly from rheumatism. He took to shooting from the back of a pony, and going round the gardens in a chair, which he used to do every Sunday after church. The gardeners took care to sweep the paths beforehand, for there, as in the hunting field, he liked things in proper order. Their only son having died of wounds in Egypt in 1917, with the approach of a second world war Sir Henry decided to give Stourhead to The National Trust, with sufficient land to support it. The gift of some 3,000 acres took effect from 1946; the remaining 2,215 acres were bequeathed to his cousin Henry Peregrine Rennie Hoare, a partner in Hoare's Bank. Thus the connection between Henry Hoare's creation and the Golden Bottle was preserved. The 6th Baronet died on Lady Day 1947, followed six hours later by his wife Alda.

The National Trust and Conservation

When The National Trust took over Stourhead in 1946 the immediate task was to ensure the long-term preservation of the woodland by felling dangerous trees, clearing and replanting. This was not helped by the havoc caused by a gale in 1953. Large numbers of enormous collapsing beech, oak, chestnut and sycamore were removed and replaced, largely with beech, but also with some chestnut, larch and hemlock. Meanwhile important steps were taken towards restoring the wider structure of the landscape and repairing the buildings. Apollo's Temple was re-roofed, and access by the Rock Bridge and underpass which had been barred was opened. A major piece of work was the rebuilding of the dam to Turner's Paddock, which had become a marsh.

In 1973 a committee was appointed to draw up a report for the conservation of the garden, based on a careful study of the historical precedents. The Report was published in 1978 and was accepted as a basis for a long-term planting policy.

Of one thing there is no question: the historical importance of the Stourhead gardens and park is as an outstanding example of a landscape garden showing the influence of William Kent in the use of buildings, and intermediate at the time of its conception between Kent and Capability Brown. At the same time ideas were changing even as it was being made; and the gardens had been enriched by the plantings of subsequent owners. In the course of time the original concept had become fragmented so that the lake area appeared to be unconnected with the other grounds. This of course was never really the case; but since the public entrance from the time of Colt Hoare had been in the village, Henry Hoare's circuit walk had been reduced to a path round the lake at one level.

Paths are not a neutral means of getting from one place to another; they direct attention. To approach the lake for the first time from above is to see it in a different perspective, as part of a larger scene whose details are gradually to be revealed. As William Shenstone said, 'the eye should always rather look down upon water.' One of the first recommendations of the Report was therefore 'that the recognised route from the main car park to the gardens should be from the direction of the house, as originally intended'. This also meant that the Fir Walk, the oldest part of Henry Hoare's scheme, long overgrown and forgotten, and now restored, could be added to the attractions of the circuit.

Some parts, such as the approaches to the house and the ground surrounding it, have changed out of all recognition since 1785. These, as well as the gravel paths extended round the north arm of the lake, the planting of the south side, on and below

Apollo's Hill, were Colt Hoare's main contribution to the grounds. Gravel paths are indeed a practical necessity; but where they cross what should be open spaces, they are a disturbing intrusion. So obtrusive paths are being moved back from the borders of the lake to the fringes of the woodland on the east and west sides.

The traditional structure of the woodland, consisting of mainly deciduous forest trees, and the collection of nineteenth- and early twentieth-century conifers which have so enriched the winter landscape, will be maintained. The modern choice of trees and shrubs is enormous; but those at Stourhead will, as far as possible, represent the taste of the various owners, except that they will be grouped and arranged with regard to the design of the landscape as a whole.

The character of the planting in evoking mood is a more subtle matter, but it is an essential part of the eighteenth-century concept; not only is there a change of level in the circuit walk, but there is the transition from garden to pastoral landscape. Horace Walpole described the Grotto as 'lost in a wood'. Joseph Spence contrasted the 'dark walk' to the Grotto with the 'soft and pleasing scenery' leading to the Pantheon. The German, C.C.L.Hirschfeld, in his *Theory of the Art of Gardens* (1785), said that after crossing the bridge, the path through the 'forest' to the Grotto was marked with stones. The classic dignity of the Pantheon, the solemn inscription on the Temple of Flora, all call for their appropriate accompaniment. But if the associations and overtones belonging to Henry Hoare's generation are perhaps beyond conservation, nevertheless there is something about great works of art which never fails to arouse a response in future generations. Despite some notable trees, Stourhead is not primarily a botanical collection; the temples are not just the ornaments of a garden, but essential to the concept at a variety of levels. The beauty of Stourhead consists in architecture, sculpture, water, plants, adapted to the natural advantages of the ground, and associated to form a work of art which is unique.

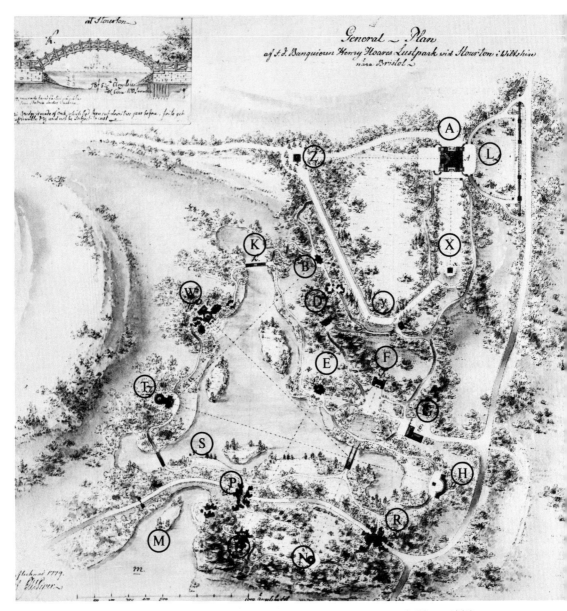

General plan of the Pleasure Garden at Stourton (with key) F.M. Piper 1779

L Lawn or grassfield in front of Villa (**A**) which slopes and enlarges towards the road with an 'ha-ha' (**T**) between the nearest pedestals.

Z Obelisk of the same dimensions as the one at Porta del Popolo in Rome.

X Statue of Apollo Belvedere on a mound at the end of a lawn 128 feet wide and four times as long on that side.[1]

y-y Terrace: where two straight walks from Apollo's statue and the Obelisk meet: and from which there is an extensive view over the lower arrangements and

[1] i.e. the south side.

the Temple of the Sun (**N**), the Hermitage (**O**) and other things on the opposite hillside.

P Vaulted steps over the road between artificial rocks to get to the Hermitage.

R Souterrain or grotto which passes under the road.

S Dam which with its concave side retains a mass of water 28 feet of depth and by means of which a triangular artificial basin or lake has been formed between the surrounding hills.

44

Buildings, Sculptures and other Monuments

The Obelisk

Built 1839–40 of Bath stone, and surmounted by a solar disc, it replaced the original of Chilmark stone, built by William Privet for Henry Hoare and begun in 1746. It was struck by lightning in 1853 and restored. The memorial tablet with a dedication to his grandfather was added by Sir Richard Colt Hoare in 1815. (Refs. Agreement with Wm Privet and others, 1746, W.R.O. 343.907; Account Books, F.S. (W.) 18 June 1747; W.R.O. 383.6, 28 Sep. 1750.)

Key to Plan *continued*

T Pantheon or Rotunda with a portico of six columns in the front and which together with four statues has cost 12,000 £ sterling.

W Grotto built against the slope of the hill on the back side consisting of many caverns and sections with accompanying *rigoles*, minor cascades, bath-cisterns and statues.

K Bridge-span of oak, 100 feet[1] of opening, with steps from both abutments and a level-plane on the top and from which a path winds up to the tent (**B**).

D Chinese alcove.

E Temple of Flora.

F Orangery.

G Gardener's Building.

H Portique.[2]

M Lower water to which the former, through the old running stream, had its outlet and to which, through the dam, three outlets direct the water from the upper lake when it needs to be emptied and which was done when building the grotto (**W**).

Obs. From z-y the walk (which is 32 feet wide) is clad with the finest turf and has on both sides 10 to 15 feet green glacis or slopes whereupon is a high and dense plantation of Cedars, Beeches and American so-called Silver Pines (because their needles look just as if they were clad with silver on the bottom side).

[1] 100 Swedish feet corresponding to 98 ft 5½ in. English; compare drawing of the bridge, top left.

[2] The Bristol Cross is not mentioned, although marked on the plan.

Obelisks are ancient Egyptian symbols for the sun's rays, when they were placed in pairs before temples and gateways. They were used as architectural features by the Romans and in the Renaissance. In England their use as park ornaments or memorials was popularized by Vanbrugh (e.g. Castle Howard, Stowe) and William Kent (Holkham, Shotover), marking a crossroads, the axis of the house or as a focal point closing a straight walk.

The Temple of Flora 1744–46

Formerly called the Temple of Ceres. Architect, Henry Flitcroft. Built by William Privet in Chilmark stone, a fine-grained limestone; a room with a portico of four detached columns of the Tuscan Doric order (i.e. the simplest form of

Temple of Flora, and Urn (*Photo, Edwin Smith*)

45

column, without fluting), metope, frieze and triangular pediment.

Over the door is the inscription *Procul, O procul este profani* ('Begone, you who are un-initiated! Begone!'), the words of the Cumaean Sybil in the *Aeneid*, Book VI, as Aeneas was about to descend into the underworld where the story of the founding of Rome was to be revealed to him. The words were inscribed in the early sixteenth century over the entrance to the Pope's private garden in the Vatican (the Belvedere).

Inside, opposite the door, is a copy of the antique **Borghese Vase** (now in the Louvre), with a relief of a Bacchanalian festival. It was made by Daniel Pincot in artificial stone, a process owned by Mrs Eleanor Coade, who set up a manufactory in London *c.*1769. She was paid for the Stourhead vase in 1772. It was originally put in the Venetian seat near the terrace above the Temple of Flora (see drawing by F.M. Piper) and was presumably moved to its present position by Colt Hoare, when the seat was pulled down in the late 1790s.

The **two marble busts,** after the antique on either side, were also moved from the Venetian seat. They represent the young Marcus Aurelius (left) and possibly Alexander the Great (right). The **circular niches** in the walls to left and right, with marble female busts, are contemporary with the building. The 'altars', in the style of William Kent, and four seats are also contemporary. The latter were copied from Bernard de Montfaucon's *Supplement to Antiquity Explained* (1725, p.41), and are early examples of archaeological correctness in English eighteenth-century furniture. A description of Stourhead in the *London Chronicle* for 18 June 1757 (anonymous, but in fact by Jonas Hanway) reads: 'Here is the figure of the Goddess (i.e. a Ceres or Flora), with her proper emblems, standing in front of you as you open the door. On each side are two commodious seats, which are made in imitation of the Pulvinaria, or little beds which were placed near the altar at the time of sacrifice, on which the pagans were wont to lay the images of their gods in their temples. Eight or ten feet below, level with the water, in a subterranean grotto, is another figure of a River God.' This was a reclining statue, bought from Thomas Manning in 1743, and placed in a niche over a spring known as Paradise Well. It was part of an architectural cascade designed by Henry Flit-

Temple of Flora, Seat (*pulvinaria*)

Engraving from Montfaucon

croft in 1744. It stood at the head of a rectangular basin or canal of much earlier date, since it is marked on a map of 1722. It was probably the village water supply. Flitcroft's temple replaced an earlier building. A drawing by C.W. Bampfylde, dated 1753, shows the scene just before the dam was completed. The lake subsequently covered the lower part of the cascade. A rocky recess is all that remains. A statue of Neptune and four horses was placed on a pedestal in the basin before the temple in 1765, but had disappeared by the first decade of the nineteenth century.

The Urn, near the rocky recess on the left of the path over the spring, is shown in a painting, *c.*1813, by Francis Nicholson, on the opposite side of the path, next to the Temple. It was moved to its present position early this century by the 6th Baronet.

The Rockwork Boathouse, to the left of the path beyond the Temple of Flora, was built by Colt Hoare and completed in 1794.

Grotto: Interior, F. Nicholson, *c.*1813

The Grotto

A circular domed chamber with two symmetrical arms; entrance and exit of simulated rustic stonework with pediments of Chilmark stone. The inscription on the pediment of the entrance, buried in a serpentine rockwork passage added in 1776, reads:

Intus aquae dulces, vivoque sedilia saxo, Nympharum domus

(Within, fresh water and seats in the living rock, the home of the nymphs)

It is taken from the *Aeneid*, Book I, where Virgil describes the cave in the haven near Carthage where Aeneas and his men take refuge from a storm. It was also inscribed on a stone seat in William Shenstone's contemporary park at The Leasowes.

The central chamber is constructed of brick, covered with tufa (waterworn limestone deposit), with a framework of stone ribs or courses. It is lighted from above by an opening in the dome. The floor is of pebbles laid in a concentric pattern. An irregular rockwork opening on one side frames a picturesque scene of the bridge and church on the far side of the lake; while opposite there is a recess with a cold bath, and the statue of a sleeping nymph over a cascade, formed by springs which flow continuously even in the driest weather. The section drawn by the Swedish artist F.M. Piper in 1779 shows how the hillside is cut away and a wall built, causing the water to rise and flow over a table of flat stones behind the nymph and fall into the bath, from where it is conveyed by drains into the lake.

The Inscription, cut in the marble on the rim of the cold bath, is a modern copy replacing the original in 1967. The words,

Nymph of the Grot these sacred springs I keep
And to the murmur of these waters sleep;
Ah! spare my slumbers, gently tread the cave,
And drink in silence or in silence lave.

are Pope's translation of a pseudo-classical poem forged in the fifteenth century, and used in conjunction with the statue of a reclining nymph in the fountains of several Italian Renaissance gardens. One such, in the garden of the Colocci family, is engraved in Montfaucon's *L'Antiquité expliquée* (1719), which is in the library at Stourhead. The Stourhead statue is a lead copy of the famous sleeping *Ariadne* which was part of the collection in the Belvedere garden of the Vatican. There were many others, the earliest being a cast at Fontainebleau (now in the Louvre) made for Francis I. In ancient Greece, Ariadne figured in the Dionysian mysteries, where she was the God's bride. Dionysus was also a god of fertility and vegetation. The Vatican statue was at one time thought to represent Cleopatra, because of a snake bracelet. Vasari, in his life of Daniello Ricciarelli of Volterra, wrote that in the time of Julius III (1550–55) the Pope 'desiring to have a fountain at the end of the corridor of the Belvedere . . . gave Daniello the task of making a grotto for the divine Cleopatra'. The Stourhead statue has no bracelet, hence Horace Walpole referred to it as 'Cleopatra without the asp'.

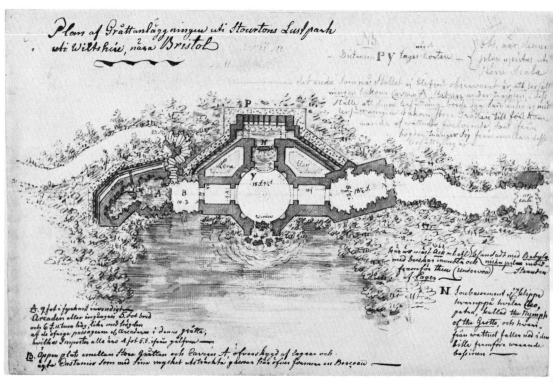

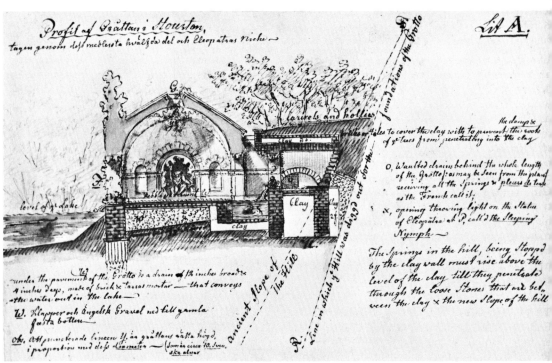

(*Top*) Grotto: Plan, F.M. Piper, 1779. (*Bottom*) Grotto: Section, F.M. Piper, 1779

(*Above*) Grotto: Nymph. (*Photo, K. Woodbridge*)

(*Right*) Nymph, Montfaucon

HVIVS NYMPHA LOCI SACRI CVSTODIA FONTIS
DORMIO DVM BLANDAE SENTIO MVRMVR AQVAE
PARCE MEVM QVISQVIS TANGIS CAVA MARMORA SOMNVM
RVMPERE SIVE BIBAS SIVE LAVERE TACE

(Refs. Alexander Pope, *Correspondence*. 1956, letter to Edward Blount, 2 June 1725; also Otto Kurz, 'Huius Nympha loci', *Journal of the Warburg and Courtauld Institute*, XVI, 1953.)

In one letter Henry Hoare referred to the Grotto as 'the temple of the nymph'; in other words a Nymphaeum, in Roman times a room furnished with fountains and statues as a refuge from the heat. They were fashionable from the sixteenth to the eighteenth centuries, often of an architectural form, but also as artificial caverns, hollowed in the rock. Important eighteenth-century English precedents for the Stourhead Grotto were Pope's grotto at Twickenham, a tunnel under the road linking his house with his garden, and covered with all kinds of exotic rock and crystal; and a grotto at Goldney House in Bristol (1739) which still exists, and has a room lined with shells and minerals, and the statue of a river god in a narrow recess.

The River God's Cave, facing the exit of the Grotto, is a rockwork construction similar to the entrance but of an earlier date. John Cheere's River God of painted lead was paid for in 1751 (W.R.O. 383.4, 7 Aug. 1751). A wooden tablet once hung before the cave with an inscription from Ovid's *Metamorphoses* describing the home of the River God Peneus in the Vale of Tempe:

*Haec domus, haec sedes, haec sunt penetralia magni
Amnis; in hoc residens facto de cantibus antro
Undis jura dabat, nymphisque colentibus undas.*

(This was the home, the dwelling, the most secret haunt of the great river. Sitting here, in a cave hewn out of the cliffs, he was dispensing justice to the waves and to the nymphs who inhabited his stream.) [Trans. M.M. Innes]

Piper's drawings show the statue with an oar held in the right hand, but attempts to fit a pole of the right dimensions in that position have proved unsuccessful. The discovery that the statue corresponds almost exactly to the figure of *Tiber* in an engraving by Salvator Rosa suggests the alternative interpretation referred to

49

River God. (*Photo, K. Woodbridge*)

Tiber and Aeneas, Salvator Rosa, Metropolitan Museum of Art, New York. (*Photo, Arts Council*)

earlier (p.19), namely that the River God is pointing in the direction of the path to the Pantheon. Compared with other garden statues, the River God is a powerful piece of modelling, and on Piper's drawing is attributed to Rysbrack. While there is no evidence for this, and from the bill, it clearly came from Cheere's workshop, in view of Rysbrack's close association with Henry Hoare there is always the possibility that he had a hand in it.

The Gothic Cottage

The Cottage is not mentioned by eighteenth-century visitors nor does it appear in Bampfylde's panoramic sketches of about 1770, or in Piper's plan of 1779. But some sort of building was evidently there, buried in the trees, as it is marked on the estate map of 1785. In 1806 Col. Hoare added the Gothic seat and porch (letter to John Carter, W.R.O. 383.907), and turned it into a feature. Nicholson's painting shows it thatched and covered with creeper. It was converted to a summer-house in 1895; and in 1907 was re-roofed with stone tiles from an old cottage at West Knoyle.

The Pantheon 1753–54
Architect, Henry Flitcroft

First called the Temple of Hercules, as it was built to house Rysbrack's statue. A portico of six Corinthian columns, with closed bays, screens, a vestibule and a domed rotunda. Pedimented niches to the right and left of the portico contain lead statues of **Bacchus** and **Venus Callipygos** probably by John Cheere. Wrought-iron gates by Benjamin Smith of Westminster, close the interior from the vestibule (F.S. Acc. 20 Dec 1761). The interior of the temple is circular with seven arched recesses, covered by a coffered dome with centre opening; immediately below the dome is a frieze of ox-skulls and garlands.

The Sculpture. Facing the entrance is Michael Rysbrack's statue of **Hercules** in marble commissioned in 1747 (agreement W.R.O. 383.4) and signed 'Mich. Rysbrack 1756'. The terracotta model (left to Henry Hoare in Rysbrack's will, and now in the Picture Gallery) was made in 1744. According to George Vertue, Rysbrack

Gothic Cottage, F. Nicholson, *c*.1813

Profil af Stora Lusthus

Façade af det Stora Lusthuset i Stourton park kalladt Pantheon

(*Top and above*) Pantheon: Section and elevation,
F. M. Piper, 1779

'finding himself somewhat at leisure, business not being so brisk . . . set himself about a model of Hercules, with the intention to show all the skill therein he was master of'. He took the antique Farnese Hercules for the proportions, but made his model standing in a different attitude with the limbs otherwise disposed. Various parts were taken from studies of famous boxers. (Ref. M.I. Webb, *Michael Rysbrack*, 1954). In October 1762 Henry Hoare wrote to his daughter Susanna (Lady Bruce), 'I thought old Rysbrack would have wept for joy to see his offspring placed to such advantage. He thinks it impossible for such a space to have more magnificence in it and striking awe than he found there.' The significance of Hercules as an ancient cult figure associated with gardens and his importance as a moral hero in the Renaissance has been described above (p.18).

On the left of Hercules, as you face the statue, is Rysbrack's **Flora,** also in marble, paid for in full in 1761 (W.R.O. 383.6, 11 Dec. 1760; 14 Dec. 1761).

Next to *Flora*, in an anticlockwise direction, is

Diana, in lead; and next to the door **St Susanna** after François Duquesnoy (called Il Fiammingo), the founder of the Flemish school of sculptors in the classical tradition, of which Rysbrack, through his father, was a member. The subject possibly had a particular association for Henry Hoare, as his wife (who died in 1743) was called Susan, and his elder daughter Susanna.

To the right of *Hercules* (clockwise) stands an antique **Livia Augusta as Ceres** in marble, much restored; **Meleager,** by John Cheere in plaster (W.R.O. 383.6, 12 Nov. 1762); and **Isis** also in plaster.

Over the niches and above the door are eight relief panels of painted plaster by Benjamin Carter (W.R.O. 383.6, 9 May 1761).

The seats, specially made for the temple, have back panels said by Horace Walpole to have been painted by William Hoare of Bath. Although Walpole says the subject was the story of **Cupid and Psyche,** this is not at present the case. Walpole was not always accurate however;

he said the inscription in front of the River God's cave was from Virgil.

The Pantheon was heated by a stove in the rear, from which warm air passed through a grille behind *Hercules*. The room and the stove are no longer there, but they are shown on Piper's plan and section of the temple in 1779; and the heating is referred to by Horace Walpole in 1762 (see p.21 above).

The Pantheon is the most important temple at Stourhead, having visual, symbolic and practical functions. It serves as a focus for the whole scene, giving it its classical character. Seen for the first time on approaching the lake, it invites movement; it is also a resting place at the point in the circuit walk where, having emerged into the open, we are invited to pause and look back at the village and the bridge across the water. The fact that it was heated shows that it was intended for retirement or entertainment, like those Italian casinos to which it is related. Finally, although Flitcroft's portico is an English Palladian concept, its intention is to recall its prototype, one of the best preserved and admired of Roman buildings.

The Iron Bridge

By Maggs and Hindley, across the southwest arm of the lake, it was erected in July 1860, replacing an oak one of 1842. There had been another before that date, of a simple post and rail type, shown in Nicholson's painting of the Pantheon and Gothic cottage.

The Dam *c.*1754

This obviously took some time to build, and was first mentioned by Henry Flitcroft in a letter to Henry Hoare (25 Aug. 1744) referring to 'a sketch of how I conceive the head of the lake should be formed'. Dr Richard Pococke in July 1754 reported 'two large pieces of water (see map 1722), which are to be made into one and much enlarged for which a head is making at great expense.'

The Cascade 1766

In fact the river Stour; that is, the water from the lake conveyed in ducts under the road, to fall into Turner's Paddock lake below the dam.

Rysbrack's *Hercules*

53

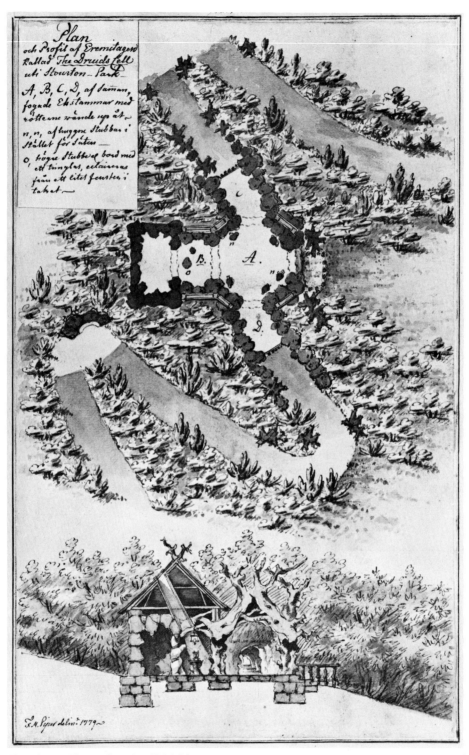

Hermitage: Plan and section, F.M. Piper, 1779

In a letter to Lord Bruce (23 Dec. 1765), Henry Hoare writes, 'Messrs Bampfield & Hoare [i.e. William Hoare of Bath] have made an ingenious model for the Cascade like Mr. Bampfield's [at Hestercombe near Taunton; see painting in the Saloon] & as I have stone quarries on the hill just above it I hope to finish it soon in the summer.'

The Rock-work Bridge

Across the Zeals road, it was probably made between 1762 and 1765. It is not mentioned by Horace Walpole; but Joseph Spence wrote to the Earl of Lincoln in September 1765, 'You go from hence, by the side of the lake and between two waters, to an odd sort of ruinous building, which hides the road; and over which you wind by roughish steps, towards the Walk of the Muses, and the Temple of Apollo.'

The Hermitage

The stone recess to the right of the zig-zag path is all that remains of The Hermitage or Druid's Cell 1771, dismantled 1814 (see letter from Henry Hoare to his granddaughter p.26). It was made of old trees. Piper's drawing shows that it had the same calculated lighting effects as the Grotto, of which in plan it was a serpentine version.

The Temple of Apollo

Designed by Henry Flitcroft, it was built in 1765 and is a round temple with detached Corinthian columns on a raised platform, and a scalloped entablature. It is a version of a round temple illustrated in Robert Wood's *Ruins of Balbec*, of which Henry Hoare bought a copy in 1757. But more probably Flitcroft was inspired by Sir William Chambers's Temple of the Sun at Kew (1761), a nearer rendering of the Balbec temple. The Stourhead temple has a circular drum with lights below the cupola. According to the Reverend R. Warner in 1801, each niche was 'filled with its deity, cast in lead from antique models. A large cast of the Belvedere Apollo occupies the interior, which is lighted from above by a circular hole. The roof of the temple spreads into a dome, and has a double ceiling; in the lower is the aperture, and in the coving

Engraving of temple from Wood's *Ruins of Balbec*, 1757

of the other, a splendid gilt representation of the Solar Rays, which, receiving the real light of this orb by an artful construction, throws into the temple below a most splendid reflection when the sun is in its strength.' The lead statues were moved to the house when it was rebuilt in 1903–04. Three are above the portico; others on the steps outside the west front. The statues at present in the temple are copies made in 1907–08 The cupola was originally a shallow hemisphere like the Pantheon; it has been replaced at least twice; the present one dates from the 1950s.

Grotto Underpass *c.*1760–65
See reference on p.23

Palladian Bridge

The stone Palladian Bridge referred to in Henry Hoare's letter of October 1762 (see p.23) is taken directly from Giacomo Leoni's translation of *The Architecture of Palladio* (1721), Book III, plate xii. The wooden bridge of one arch (sometimes incorrectly called 'Chinese', even by

55

Temple of Apollo, F.Nicholson, *c.*1813

The Bristol High Cross, S.H.Grimm, 1790

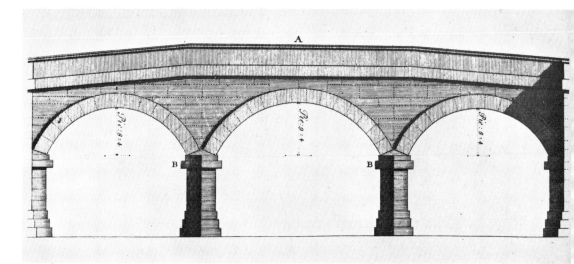

Bridge, Palladio

Colt Hoare), which crossed the north arm of the lake, was from the same book, plate vi.

The Bristol High Cross

Erected at Stourhead in 1765, this is a medieval monument of several dates, the oldest part being early fifteenth-century. The cross originally stood at the junction of High Street and Broad Street in Bristol. It was removed as an obstruction in 1733, rebuilt on College Green three years later, and finally dismantled in 1762. The circumstances of the cross's arrival at Stourhead are described above (p.24).

Recent research (M.J.H.Liversidge, *The Bristol High Cross*, Bristol 1978) has thrown doubt on some of the accepted early history. What may safely be said is that the lower tiers are of early fifteenth-century origin; that these were extensively restored, and a new finial added, in 1525. In 1633 it was again renovated, and the height increased by a new tier of seated figures representing Henry VI, Queen Elizabeth, James I and Charles I (the last was removed under the Commonwealth in 1651, and replaced after the Restoration). Of the older statues in the lower tier, three traditionally represent King John, Henry III and Edward I. It is suggested that the fourth, being contemporary in style with the others, represents Edward I, and not Edward IV as it was thought formerly.

The removal of the cross to Stourhead necessi-tated a solid base, instead of the elegant central pier which was badly decayed. The structure was further strengthened by iron dowels which have damaged the stonework. It was restored in 1894; and in 1979 was again unstable. It was taken down, and re-erected in 1981. The iron dowels are now replaced by stainless steel. It now stands on five shafts as originally intended, as the infilled base is no longer regarded as necessary for stability. The four standing figures in the lower tier were too fragile to be repaired. They are loaned to the Victoria and Albert Museum, in return for carved stone replicas.

St Peter's Church

This does not belong to the Trust, but forms part of Henry Hoare's picturesque scene.

The interior has fourteenth-century arcades which were altered in 1847 when the church was reconstructed, a new aisle thrown out, a vestry added, and a clock put in the tower. It was re-roofed and rearranged in 1877. The east window was removed in 1937.

The most interesting features are the monu-ments. Opposite the north door the mutilated figure of a lady *c*.1400; and in the wall above the arcade, two memorials of interest: one to Nathaniel Ireson, the master mason who built the house; the other to Francis Faugoin, Henry Hoare's steward, responsible for supervising all the work of construction in the garden. In the

north aisle is a tomb chest with recumbent effigies of the 6th Lord Stourton (d.1536) and his wife.

The Hoare monuments in the south aisle are fine examples of period styles. The memorial to the first Henry Hoare is architectural, with urns left and right, Corinthian columns, and an open pediment surmounted by a bust. His son's (Henry Hoare II, d.1785) is an asymmetrical composition in white and brown marble by Charles Harris, with two putti by an urn. Colt Hoare's memorial to his wife Hester (d.1785) is in a neo-classical style: a pink granite sarcophagus on a tall base, surmounted by a black granite urn (an early use of granite). In the churchyard is Sir Richard Colt Hoare's tomb, a marble sarcophagus (ordered from Florence in 1819) under a Gothic canopy with a pierced parapet.

St Peter's Pump 1474

This was erected in Six Wells Bottom on a grotto base in 1768 (dated) over the first springs

(*Left*) St Peter's Pump, engraving J.Greig
(*Below*) The Convent

of the Stour. It formerly stood near St Peter's Church at the west corner of Peter Street, Bristol, and was removed by Act of Parliament in 1766. The nearest approach to it is from the top of the valley on the road to Alfred's Tower.

The Convent

In the woods below the Tower is the Convent (probably 1760–70), an irregular rustic building in a Gothic style with thatched roof, turrets and spires. *The building is not open to the public.*

Alfred's Tower

Designed by Henry Flitcroft, it stands on King-settle Hill two miles north-west of Stourhead House, on the edge of the escarpment overlooking the Somerset plain. It is the culmination of the outer circuit, starting on the terrace ride along the north side of Six Wells Bottom. It was designed by Henry Flitcroft, who had previously built such a tower at Wentworth Woodhouse, Yorkshire, in 1748. The project for the Tower was conceived in 1762 and commemorates the peace with France, and the succession two years previously of George III, like Alfred 'a truly British king'. The Stourhead tower is a triangular brick structure 160 feet high, with round projections at the corners, one of which contains a staircase leading to a platform with a crenellated parapet. The interior is hollow and open to the sky. Its only ornaments are three horizontal stone bands, a statue of King Alfred in the Gothic taste and an inscription. Several drafts are recorded: the final version on the Tower is:

Alfred the Great
A.D. 879 on this summit
Erected his standard against the Danish Invaders
To Him we owe
The origin of Juries
The Establishment of a Militia
the Creation of a Naval Force
Alfred the light of a benighted age
was a Philosopher and a Christian
The Father of his People
The Founder of the English
Monarchy and Liberty

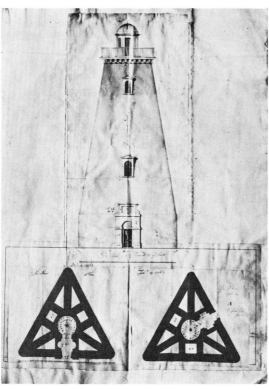

(*Left, top*) Alfred's Tower, drawing, 1784

(*Left*) Design for tower at Wentworth Woodhouse by Henry Flitcroft, 1748. (*Photo, Architectural Review*)

Planting 1741–1946

Note: This section is intended as a historical guide to the trees planted by owners *before* the National Trust. For a complete guide to the present collection please refer to *Mature Trees in the Stourhead Landscape*, National Trust 1981.

1720-1785

There are no records of trees planted by Henry Hoare II apart from notes on F.M.Piper's sketches (1778), Colt Hoare's *Memoirs*, and some references by visitors. On the whole his range was restricted. His thoughts on planting, reported by Joseph Spence, were:

The greens should be ranged in large masses as the shades are in painting, to contrast the *dark* masses with the *light* ones, and to relieve each dark mass itself with little sprinklings of lighter greens here and there.

His difficulty was in finding evergreens for the dark accents. Colt Hoare said that the woodland was a mixture of beech and fir, which in the nomenclature of the time included the spruce family. Piper refers to American silver pine ('Americanske silvera furar') in the Fir Walk, which could be *Picea glauca* (white spruce) introduced from North America in 1700. On the other hand, Sir John Parnell (1768) identified them as 'Spruce Fir'. Weeping willow was planted on the shore near the Grotto; and common laurel was used as underplanting.

List 1. *Trees existing in 1741 or planted by Henry Hoare II*

Genus	Species	Common name	Introduced England	Stourhead	Reference
BROAD-LEAVED TREES					
ACER	campestre	Field maple	N		S654
—	platanoides	Norway maple	N		F441,M559,Z708
—	pseudoplatanus	Sycamore	N		Q
ALNUS	glutinosa	Alder	N		H480,K534
CASTANEA	sativa	Spanish chestnut	N		A995,B759,I497,J514
FAGUS	sylvatica	Common beech	N		Q
FRAXINUS	excelsior	Common ash	N		
QUERCUS	robur	Common oak	N		Q
—	ilex	Holm oak	16th C		C812,G435

| | | N = Native | | Q = Quantity |

Bridge, lake and south bank, C.W. Bampfylde, *c.*1770, Stourhead Library

Bridge and south bank, F. Nicholson, *c.*1813

New planting along path on east side of lake, F. Nicholson, panorama (detail) *c.*1812,

Bridge and south bank, nineteenth-century conifers. (*Photo K.Woodbridge*)

Genus	Species	Common name	Introduced England	Stourhead	Reference
CONIFEROUS TREES					
CEDRUS	*libani*	Cedar of Lebanon	*c.*1645		E376,W561,Z574
LARIX	*decidua (europaea)*	Common larch	*c.*1620		O502
PICEA	*abies (excelsa)*	Common or Norway spruce	*c.*1500		N461
TAXUS	*baccata*	Yew	N		Q
			N=Native		Q=Quantity

1785-1838

Many of Sir Richard Colt Hoare's nurserymen's bills have been preserved; and he recorded some of his planting in the *Stourhead Annals*. He introduced new ornamental species, but many are not now represented; for instance only three of the eight species of maple, and four out of some dozen species of oak. He favoured broad-leaved trees, especially in the woodland, from which he removed Henry Hoare's conifers, cutting down the Fir Walk. He introduced *Rhododendron ponticum* in 1791, and in 1828 planted a large number of an unspecified species (possibly *R. catawbiense* which had been introduced into England in 1809). Two *R. arboreum* were ordered in 1834. He greatly increased the amount of common laurel as underplanting; and some fifty species of hardy or half hardy shrubs are listed in nurserymen's bills. (See Woodbridge, *Garden History*, IV, No 1, 1976.) At least half were probably intended for the conservatory. The gardener's house, remodelled in 1808–9, and shown in Francis Nicholson's painting, has a verandah covered with some climbing plant; the Gothic Watch Cottage too. Those listed are clematis (eight varieties), honeysuckle, ivy, jasmine, *Rosa banksiae* and *Rosa multiflora*.

List 2. *Trees introduced by Sir Richard Colt Hoare 1791–1838*

Genus	Species	Common name	Introduced England	Stourhead	Reference
ACER	*negundo*	Box elder	*c.*1688	1791	I499
—	*rubrum*	Red maple	1656		436
—	*saccharinum*	Silver maple	1735	1791	G433,O573,Q594, W690
—	*pseudoplatanus* 'Variegatum'	Variegated sycamore	1730	1791	C443,N566,Y701

Genus		Species	Common name	Introduced England	Stourhead	Reference
AESCULUS		hippocastanum	Horse chestnut	E 17th C		J519
—	×	carnea	Pink horse chestnut	E 17th C	1833	Y695
—		octandra (*flavia*)	Sweet buckeye	1764	1791	F456
BETULA		pendula	Silver or common birch	N		K537,L531,Q597
CATALPA		bignonioides	Indian bean tree	1726	1791	B821
CELTIS		occidentalis	Hackberry (Nettle tree)	1656	1791	
CRATAEGUS		mollis	Red hawthorn		1811	F462
FRAXINUS		excelsior 'Pendula'	Weeping ash		1791	G415
—		ornus	Manna ash	17th C	1791	E403,E477,S630, S642,S644,S645,T656, U675,Y697
ILEX		aquifolium	Common holly	N		
LIRIODENDRON		tulipifera	Tulip tree	c.1688	1791	B765,B769,B770, B763,G429,K536, Q600,S630,S665, U677,V676,V683
LIQUIDAMBAR		styraciflua	Sweet gum	17th C	1791	C795,C784,Q605
PHILLYREA		latifolia		1597	1791	O03
PLATANUS	×	hispanica	London plane	c.1663	1791	H469,R622
—		orientalis	Oriental plane	E 16th C	1817	719
PRUNUS		avium	Wild cherry	N	1791	L543,N568,O575
—		avium 'Plena'	Double gean	since 1700	1791	969
QUERCUS		cerris	Turkey oak	1735	1807	B820,J509,P592
—		coccinea	Scarlet oak	1691	1791	837
—		palustris	Pin oak	1800	1813	741
—		phellos	Willow oak	1723	1813	C790
ROBINIA		pseudoacacia	Locust tree or false acacia	17th C	1791	L548
TILIA		americana	American lime	1752	1791	R620, W690
—	×	europaea	Common lime	N		J956,R617
—		platyphyllos	Broad-leaved lime	N	1791	F439

CONIFEROUS TREES

Genus	Species	Common name	Introduced England	Stourhead	Reference
TAXODIUM	distichum	Deciduous or swamp cypress	c.1640		Q528

N = Native

1838-1894

The lifetime of the 3rd, 4th and 5th Baronets, covering most of Queen Victoria's reign, was a period when many new species of trees were introduced into England. Discoveries by Archibald Menzies, David Douglas and William Lobb gave a new character to many parts of the English landscape, nowhere more than at Stourhead.

From 1838 to 1857 about twenty new species of conifer were added to the collections, including the first specimens of Douglas fir and hemlock spruce, which were later widely used in commercial plantations. Giant species such as *Thuja plicata* (western red cedar) made their appearance; as well as strange trees like the monkey puzzle (*Araucaria araucana*) introduced by Lobb from Chile in 1844. Although the *Stourhead Annals* were discontinued from 1860 to 1894, it is evident from the estimated age of existing trees that at least fourteen varieties were added in that period, including Lawson cypress, Wellingtonia and Sitka spruce.

List 3. *Conifers: Nineteenth-century introductions now represented at Stourhead*

Genus	Species	Common name	Introduced England	Stourhead	Reference
ABIES	nordmanniana	Caucasian fir	1840	c.1872	F398,M453,N464
—	procera	Noble fir	1830	1850–60	G387,G388,N463, O509,P518,P525
—	procera 'Glauca'		1863		H402
ARAUCARIA	araucana	Monkey puzzle	1844	1852–3	I418,N485,N462, N510,W562
CALOCEDRUS	decurrens	Incense cedar	1853		459
CEDRUS	atlantica	Atlas cedar	c.1840	1854–5	J429
—	atlantica 'Glauca'	Blue cedar	c.1840	c.1872	F394
—	deodara	Deodar	1831	1852–3	R534
CHAMAECYPARIS	lawsoniana	Lawson cypress	1854	c.1872	H404,L441,L443, L444,N486,Q531, Z572
—	nootkatensis	Nootka cypress	1853	1855–60	F377,H413,I417, N466,O501
—	pisifera 'Filifera'	Sawara cypress	1861	c.1872	
—	pisifera 'Squarrosa' Aurea'		1889		U550
CRYPTOMERIA	japonica	Japanese cedar	1842	c.1882	F397,P524,V579
PICEA	polita	Tiger-tail spruce	1861	c.1872	W558
—	sitchensis	Sitka spruce	1831	1862	H408,I415,N469
PINUS	parviflora	Japanese white pine	1861	c.1861–4	I419,N476
—	peuce	Macedonian pine	1864		H405,N495
—	pinaster	Maritime pine	16th C		N479
—	wallichiana (excelsa)	Bhutan pine	c.1823	1851–3	K435
PSEUDOTSUGA	menziesii	Douglas fir	1827	1854–5	J424,J428,N490,Y567

List 3. *continued*

Genus	Species	Common name	Introduced England	Stourhead	Reference
SEQUOIA	sempervirens	Coast redwood	1843	1852–3	H514,P564,Y564
SEQUOIADENDRON	giganteum	Wellingtonia	1853	c.1862	H412,K439,W555
THUJA	plicata	Western red cedar	1853	c.1854–60	F379,O500,Q530, Y565,Y566
THUJOPSIS	dolobrata	Hiba	1853	c.1882	S539
TSUGA	heterophylla	Western hemlock	1851	1852–5	B961,F396,K434, N483,R537,W554

1894-1946

The 6th Baronet added enormously to the ornamental planting, particularly in the collection of conifers. He cleared much of the laurel, substituting new flowering shrubs; substantial introductions were made in 1901–3, 1906–9, 1912–14, and every year from 1920 to 1933. Three hundred azaleas were brought from Longleat in 1901–2; and in 1913–14 the south side of the lake, below the Temple of Apollo, was cleared and planted with new varieties of rhododendron and azalea from Messers Vuyk and Sons of Holland. It was not until 1922 that a systematic substitution of 'good hybrids' for 'common rhododendron' was recorded in the *Annals*. This went on yearly round the lake until 1938; in the Shades from 1927–33; also in the drive in 1926–7; and on the west and south lawns 1920–1, 1927–8, 1930–5.

List 4. *Trees at Stourhead introduced by the 6th Baronet*

Genus	Species	Common name	Introduced England	Stourhead	Reference
BROAD-LEAVED TREES					
ACER	griseum	Paper-bark maple	1901	1941	E401,G424,425
—	grosseri var. hersii	Snake-bark maple	c.1923		F463
—	negundo californicum	Box elder		1927	
—	palmatum	Japanese maple	1820	1927	B818,C800,C818, F449,G426,G434, I500,T664
—	palmatum purpureum			1927	
—	pseudoplatanus 'Purpureum'			1927	W686
—	rufinerve	Grey budded snake-bark maple	1879	1927	570,574
AILANTHUS	altissima	Tree of Heaven	1751		H479,S635,T657

List 4. *continued*

Genus		Species	Common name	Introduced England	Stourhead	Reference
BETULA		pendula 'Youngii'		c.1900	1931	
CERCIDIPHYLLUM		japonicum		1881	1925	B757,B768,F466, G423,T658,T659
CLADRASTIS		sinensis	Chinese yellow-wood	1901		Q606
CORNUS		nuttallii		1835	1935	406,407,455
DAVIDIA		involucrata (vilmoriniana)	Dove tree (Handkerchief tree)	1897	1935	F409,I489,Z720
FAGUS		sylvatica heterophylla 'Aspleniifolia'	Fern-leaved beech	1820		R625
HAMAMELIS		mollis	Wych-hazel	1879	1927	
IDESIA		polycarpa		c.1864		D839
LABURNUM		alpinum	Scotch laburnum	1877		506,525,824
MAGNOLIA		hypoleuca	Japanese big-leaf maple	1865	1931	
—		soulangiana		E 19th C	1927	
—		soulangiana 'Alexandrina'		E 19th C	c.1945	
—	×	soulangiana 'Lennei'			1935	
—		tripetala		1752	1931	
MALUS		floribunda	Japanese crab	1862	c.1920	G432
—		tschonoskii		1892		
POPULUS		canadensis robusta		1895		Q611
—	×	canadensis 'Serotina Aurea'	Golden poplar	1871	1927	Y704
—		canescens	Grey poplar	N	c.1905	L539,L540
—		szechuanica		1908	1927	
—	×	trichocarpa	Black cottonwood (Western balsam poplar)	1892	c.1905	L542
PRUNUS		cerasifera 'Pissardii'		1880	1927	
—		sargentii		1890	1935	
—		yedoensis chidare yoshino				693
QUERCUS		canariensis (mirbeckii)	Algerian oak (Mirbeck's oak)	c.1845		Q610
—		coccinea splendens			1940	
—		rubra (borealis maxima)	Red oak	1720	1934	C787,C788,C792, J517,K532,L553, O581,S631,X728
SALIX		alba	White willow	N	c.1900	Q603
—		alba 'Britzensis'	Scarlet willow		c.1900	

N = Native

Genus	Species	Common name	Introduced England	Stourhead	Reference
SORBUS	*aria* 'Decaisneana' ('Majestica')	Whitebeam	N		B778
TRACHYCARPUS	*fortunei*	Chusan palm	1836		R615
CONIFEROUS TREES					
ABIES	*amabilis*	Red fir	1830	1935	
—	*delavayi* 'Fabri'	Delavay's silver fir	1901	c.1905	F395
—	*delavayi* 'Forrestii'		1844	c.1925	H411
—	*firma*	Momi fir	1861	1935	L451
—	*koreana*	Korean fir	1905	1938	P522
—	*nephrolepis*	East Siberian fir	1851		
—	*spectabilis*	Himalayan fir	1822	1935	N497
—	*veitchii*	Veitch's silver fir	1879	c.1894	N480
CEPHALOTAXUS	*harringtonia* 'Fastigiata'	Cow's tail pine	1861	c.1900	W552
CHAMAECYPARIS	*lawsoniana* 'Erecta'	Lawson cypress	1855		L440
—	*lawsoniana* 'Fraseri'	Lawson cypress	1893	c.1900	T542
—	*lawsoniana* 'Intertexta'	Lawson cypress	c.1869	1930	N482
—	*lawsoniana* 'Stewartii'	Lawson cypress	1920	c.1930	P519
—	*lawsoniana* 'Triomphe de Boskoop'	Lawson cypress	c.1890	1906–7	M452
—	*lawsoniana* 'Westermannii'	Lawson cypress	c.1880		M457
—	*lawsoniana* 'Wisselii'	Lawson cypress	1888	1919	I422,P520,Z573
CRYPTOMERIA	*japonica* 'Lobbii'	Japanese red cedar	c.1850	c.1930	M454
CUNNINGHAMIA	*lanceolata*	Chinese fir	1804	1931	N481,O506
CUPRESSUS	*macrocarpa* 'Lutea'	Monterey cypress	1892	1906–7	Y563
GINGKO	*biloba*	Maidenhair tree	1727	c.1900	J430
JUNIPERUS	*squamata* 'Meyeri'	Flaky juniper	1914	1934	F393
LARIX	*decidua* 'Pendula'		1836		U549
PICEA	*abies* 'Nana Compacta'	Norway spruce	c.1855		H401
—	*abies* 'Pendula Inversa'	Norway spruce	1855	c.1930	Z571
—	*brachytyla*	Sargent spruce	1901		P523
—	*jezoensis* var. *hondoensis*	Hondo spruce	1861	c.1890	O499

N = Native

List 4. *continued*

Genus	Species	Common name	Introduced England	Stourhead	Reference
PICEA	*omorika*	Serbian spruce	1889	*c.*1922	N538
—	*orientalis*	Oriental spruce	1839		N477,N581
—	*pungens* 'Glauca'	Blue spruce	*c.*1885	1906–7	P513
—	*pungens* 'Specki' (Glauca group)			1930	
—	*smithiana*	West Himalayan spruce	1818		M456,N575
PINUS	*cembra*	Arolla pine	*c.*1746	*c.*1930	U548
—	*ponderosa*	Western yellow pine	1826		
TAXUS	*baccata aurea*	Golden yew	*c.*1855		H403
THUJA	*plicata* 'Zebrina'	Western red cedar	1868	1907	G389

Selected Stourhead Bibliography

Eighteenth and early nineteenth centuries

1754 Richard Pococke, *Travels through England*, ed. J.J.Cartwright (1889)

1755 Jonas Hanway, 'A Journal of Eight Days Journey from *Portsmouth* to *Kingston-on-Thames...* August 1755'. Serialized in the *London Chronicle*, 1757 (Stourhead, 18 June)

1762 Horace Walpole, 'Visits to Country Seats', Walpole Society, XVI, 1927–8

1765 Joseph Spence, letter to the Earl of Lincoln, 17 September 1765 (Ms. Ne C 2951, Nottingham University). Printed in Hunt and Willis, op. cit.; and *The Conservation of the Gardens at Stourhead*

1769–83 Sir John Parnell, Ms. 'Journal of a tour thro' Wales and England', anno 1769 (–1783) (see below, *Journal of Garden History*, Vol. II, No. 1, 1982)

1773 Maria Rishton, Letter to Fanny Burney, 13 April. *The Early Diary of Francis Burney*, 1768–1778. Ed. Annie Rame Ellis, Vol II, 1913

1775 William Gilpin, *Observations on the Western parts of England*, published 1798

1775 C.C.L.Hirschfeld, *Theorie der Gartenkunst*, Leipzig, 1775, V, 41

1776 Mrs Lybbe Powys, *Passages from the Diaries of Mrs. Lybbe Powys*, E.J.Climenson, ed. (1889)

1779 Anon, *A Ride and a Walk through Stourhead* (verse), London

1800 Sir Richard Colt Hoare, *Description of the House and Gardens at Stourhead*, Salisbury, 1800

1801 R.Warner, *Excursions from Bath*, 'Stourhead and Stourton'

1801 John Britton, *The Beauties of Wiltshire* II

1811 (Richard Fenton) 'A Barrister', *A Tour in Search of Genealogy*

1818 Sir Richard Colt Hoare, *A Guide to Stourhead and Desmesnes*

1822 Sir Richard Colt Hoare *History of Modern Wiltshire*, 'Hundred of Mere'

Twentieth century

There are references to Stourhead of varying accuracy in many books and articles on gardening and landscape. Those listed below are the more authoritative.

1938 Christopher Hussey, 'The Gardens of Stourhead', *Country Life* LXXXIII

1948–68 J.Lees-Milne, *Stourhead*, The National Trust Guidebook

1963 Nikolaus Pevsner, *The Buildings of England*, *Wiltshire*, Harmondsworth, revised 1975

1965 Kenneth Woodbridge, 'Henry Hoare's Paradise', *The Art Bulletin*, New York, March

1967 Christopher Hussey, *English Gardens and Landscapes 1700–1750*, London

1968 Kenneth Woodbridge, 'The Sacred Landscape: Painters and the Lake Garden of Stourhead', *Apollo*, September

1970 Kenneth Woodbridge, *Landscape and Antiquity: Aspects of English Culture at Stourhead 1718 to 1838*, Oxford. This book contains a full bibliography of source material

1970 Kenneth Woodbridge, *The Stourhead Landscape*, The National Trust, 1st edition

1974 Kenneth Woodbridge, 'The Dream of Aeneas. A Rosa Source for Cheere's River God at Stourhead', *The Burlington Magazine*, December

1976 Kenneth Woodbridge, 'The Planting of Ornamental Shrubs at Stourhead: a History, 1746 to 1946', *Garden History*, IV, No 1

1978 The National Trust, *The Conservation of the Gardens at Stourhead*, Report and Recommendations

1979 Ronald Paulson, *Emblem and Expression: Meaning in English Art of the Eighteenth Century*, Cambridge, Mass.
and
1979 James Turner, 'The Structure of Henry Hoare's Stourhead', *Art Bulletin*, March, contain speculative alternatives as to the significance of the iconography.
1982 Sir John Parnell, 'Stourhead in 1768', an unpublished account from his *Journal*, in *Journal of Garden History*, Vol. II, No.1.

Oaks Colloquium on the History of Landscape Architecture, No.2., 1974

Of general histories putting the English landscape garden in a world context, one of the more recent is Christopher Thacker, *The History of Gardens*, 1979. Miles Hadfield, *Landscape with Trees*, 1967, is an all-too-rare general history of planting. Barbara Jones, *Follies & Grottoes*, 1974, surveys the course of fashion in such buildings, with a gazetteer of existing examples. Finally, Graham S. Thomas, *Gardens of the National Trust*, 1979, writes from personal experience as The National Trust's Gardens Consultant.

General Reading

John Dixon Hunt and Peter Willis ed., *The Genius of the Place: the English Landscape Garden 1620–1820*, an anthology of 17th- and 18th-century writing with an introductory essay. The most useful general guide to the literature

Christopher Hussey, *The Picturesque: Studies in a point of view*, 1927 (reprinted 1967), and B. Sprague Allen, *Tides in English Taste*, 1937 (reprint 1969) are important pioneering studies of the cultural background. Others are Edward Malins, *English Landscaping and Literature 1660–1840*, 1966, and Walter John Hipple Jr, *The Beautiful, the Sublime and the Picturesque*, 1957, a critical study of the aesthetic theory

Sir Nikolaus Pevsner, 'The Genesis of the Picturesque', *Architectural Review* XCVI, 1944 (*Studies in Art, Architecture and Design*, 1968) and Frank Clark, *The English Landscape Garden*, 1948, have been influential on the modern historical approach

Dorothy Stroud, *Capability Brown*, 1950 (new edition 1975), and *Humphry Repton*, 1962; Peter Willis, *Charles Bridgeman and the English Landscape Garden*, 1977; Edward Malins and the Knight of Glin, *Lost Demesnes: Irish Landscape Gardening 1660–1845*, 1976; A.A. Tait, *The Landscape Garden in Scotland 1735–1835*, 1980, are important scholarly monographs on selected aspects of the subject. Others are included in *Furor Hortensis: Essays on the History of the English Landscape Garden*, ed. P. Willis, 1974, and *The Picturesque Garden*, ed. N. Pevsner, papers given at the Dumbarton